LA MIA CUCINA TOSCANA

LA MIA CUCINA TOSCANA

A TUSCAN COOKS IN AMERICA

Pino Luongo,
Andrew Friedman, and Marta Pulini

Photographs by Michele Tabozzi

Broadway Books
New York

LA MIA CUCINA TOSCANA.
Copyright © 2003 by Pino Luongo and Andrew Friedman.

PRINTED IN JAPAN

Visit our website at www.broadwaybooks.com

Book design by Elizabeth Rendfleisch
Photography by Michele Tabozzi
www.tabozzi.com

Library of Congress Cataloging-in-Publication Data
Pino, Luongo.
La mia cucina toscana : a Tuscan cooks in America / Pino Luongo,
with Marta Pulini and Andrew Friedman
p.   cm.
Includes index.
ISBN 0-7679-1194-6 (alk. paper)
1. Cookery, Italian—Tuscan style.   2. Cookery—United States.
I. Pulini, Marta.   II. Friedman, Andrew, 1967–   III. Title.

TX723.2.T86P55 2003
641.5945'5—dc21
2002043864

1 2 3 4 5 6 7 8 9 10

acknowledgments

I'd like to thank a few people for their invaluable participation in this project:

My agent, Judith Weber, for her help in devising the concept and her advice at every step of the way

Stephen Rubin, publisher of Doubleday Broadway, for his ongoing support

Jennifer Josephy, my editor at Broadway Books, for her guidance and suggestions

Jackie Everly-Warren, marketing director of Doubleday Broadway, for her creative advice

Laura Marshall of Broadway Books for her invaluable help

And the marketing and public relations department of Broadway Books for supporting this project after the writing, recipe testing, and editing were completed

contents

"Rules were made to be broken."

ANONYMOUS

introduction

If you love classic cuisine, this is a book for you. If you're a nonconformist who likes to try something original every time you set foot in the kitchen, this is a book for you. How can both of these statements be true? Because the recipes in this book take time-honored dishes, flavor combinations, and culinary concepts—both Italian and American—and adapt them to my personal taste. The result is what I like to call La Mia Cucina Toscana, or My Tuscan Cuisine.

My Tuscan Cuisine is based on my memories of Tuscan cooking, my travels in Italy, and the two decades I've spent in New York City. It is perhaps most easily explained by my telling you a bit about myself.

Up until the time I was twenty-five there was one thing you could say about me for sure: I was Italian. I was born in Florence and raised in Tuscany. As a young adult I acted in the theater in Rome. I had never been to the United States. I didn't even know how to speak English.

In my formative years I was nourished on a diet of traditional Tuscan food, much of which was the source of some of my fondest memories: coming home from school to find that my mother had prepared a refreshing bruschetta (she rubbed tomato into slices of country bread and chilled them) to hold me over until dinner or, years later, driving to a hillside café with my teenage friends and eating the quintessential Tuscan springtime snack—fava beans and Pecorino Toscano cheese—in the middle of nowhere on the first day of spring. Then there were the pasta carbonara parties we threw when I was working as an actor in Rome. After our Saturday night performance we would have a get-together where we took turns treating one another to a personal version of that dish.

Food is integral to the life of any Italian, whether he comes from Tuscany, Sicily, Milan, or Rome. We love food. We take pride in our regional recipes. We go through life measuring all food against our mothers' home cooking. And we don't think anyone can do it as well as we can. They might be able to do other things better, but we all believe that we are blessed to have been raised on the best food in the world. And we wouldn't trade it for anything.

So if I love Italy so much, what am I doing in New York City? I've been here since 1981, more than twenty years. And I love it. Shortly after I arrived, I traded in my acting career for a different kind of theatrical pursuit: I became a restaurateur.

When I opened my first restaurant, Il Cantinori, in 1983, the food was Tuscan through and through, just like me—crostini, ribollita, bistecca Fiorentina, and so on. Very satisfying, basic food you might find anywhere in Tuscany. At the time, that was enough to be original in Manhattan because nobody else was doing it. We developed an enormous following by essentially replicating the atmosphere and menu of a Tuscan trattoria on West 10th Street in New York City.

Now, here in the twenty-first century, I still speak with an Italian accent, but much has changed. I am constantly reminded of it by the little details that define my daily life. I keep track of my appointments on a Palm Pilot. I make business calls on a speakerphone in my car. My kids speak with an American accent. In other words, I've become something else: an Italian soul living an American life.

And, because restaurants are a reflection of the restaurateur's soul, the same is true of the food on my menus. And that's what this book is all about.

A CULINARY RENAISSANCE:
NEW YORK CITY IN THE 1980s AND 1990s
As much as I love traditional Italian food, I've come to realize something looking at it from the vantage point of the United States: it's awfully predictable, especially coming from such a spontaneous people. Italians are incredibly tolerant, but not when it comes to food. The core dishes in each region of Italy have remained the same for generations. If you don't believe me, spend a week in Tuscany and see how similar the menu at each restaurant is to all the others. Or visit Venice and try to find a place that doesn't specialize in grilled whole fish, filleted tableside and served with a drizzle of olive oil and a squeeze of lemon. Visiting the Cinque Terre? Then I hope you like pesto, because you're going to be eating a lot of it.

I developed this point of view because I became a New York City restaurateur during the 1980s, when American chefs were experimenting in unprecedented ways with classic French cuisine, weaving in influences from Italy, South America, and the Far East.

To me this movement in food was the contemporary, culinary equivalent of the Renaissance—a time when Tuscan artists, encouraged by patrons such as the Medici, began looking forward, taking a fresh look at art and science in a cosmopolitan city full of open-minded people who welcomed their new ideas. These artists broke time-honored conventions, taking bold steps into the future.

This distinctly American attitude toward food was a revelation. I started to look at classic Tuscan dishes and wonder how I could reinvent them, turning them into something new that still had the integrity of the original. Rather than blindly following the "rules," I began to experiment freely for an audience eager to try and appreciate new things. Not only did I adapt Tuscan cuisine, but I began to take a fresh look at the food I had experienced in other parts of Italy and, in time, to experiment with the American and international dishes I was getting to know here in New York. I call my new recipes La Mia Cucina Toscana because there's one constant in everything I do: it *feels* Tuscan. This is true whether I'm putting a new spin on a Tuscan classic or taking a dish from Rome, Sicily, or America and "Tuscanizing" it.

The results have been exciting and far-reaching. For example, over the years American ingredients have become a major part of my cooking. (When I say *my* cooking, I'm talking about the recipes I've created with my corporate chef, Marta Pulini, who is my recipe collaborator in this book as well.) When I say "American ingredients," I am referring to all of the influences that one encounters in the United States, from indigenous foods like soft-shell crabs, cranberries, and Yukon Gold potatoes to imported, ethnic favorites like lemongrass, ginger, cilantro, and so on.

But more than that, once I got going, I simply loosened up and opened myself up to the idea of trying new things. I would try to turn a traditional recipe into something completely different by altering the ratio of one ingredient to another or to take a dish from one category into another—a pasta into a soup, a roast into a salad, a side dish into a main course, and so on.

There are examples of what I'm talking about throughout the menus at all of my restaurants. If you look through the menu at Le Madri, you'll see such nontraditional dishes as our confit di coniglio (rabbit confit) appetizer and insalata di farro ai funghi (salad of farro and mushrooms). At Tuscan Square you'll find insalata di cetrioli e anguria (watermelon and cucumber salad) and tagliarini alla chitarra con polpette (tagliarini with meatballs). And at my newest restaurant, Centolire, you'll find a cacciucco (Tuscan fish stew) topped with a bread crust that's baked over the bowl.

Another example from Centolire is orata portercole, in which we crust sea bream with potatoes—a classic recipe. But we've added a distinctly modern twist: we put Pecorino cheese between the fish and the potatoes. This doesn't create a cheesy result, but rather the cheese melts away, leaving only its unique salinity behind. You will almost never find fish and cheese on the same plate in Italy, and, again, that's what makes this an example of La Mia Cucina Toscana.

Sometimes I would also look back to the past for inspiration, another similarity to the Renaissance: just as one of the inspirations for this creative era was the rediscovery of classical texts and humanist documents, one of the inspirations for me has been the rediscovery of ancient Tuscan recipes. For example, the Pichi Pachi dessert on page 247, which features slices of eggplant cooked in chocolate, is actually based on a recipe that dates back to the eighteenth century. And the same is true of the Tagliatelle Torta with Apples and Raisins on page 249. Sometimes nothing is more compelling than a rediscovered classic.

In these pages I'll share my very personal recipes, for both those dishes that have been served in my restaurants and those I have created at home through improvisation. If my first book was *A Tuscan in the Kitchen,* then this one might have been called "A Tuscan in New York," a collection of recipes written by someone who looks at food through a Tuscan lens but now lives in the melting pot of Manhattan.

I hope that this book will introduce you to a new and exciting world of food inspired by the most popular cuisine on earth. My goal is for it to teach you what I think is the most valuable lesson in any kitchen: there are no rules other than one's own personal taste and style. Armed with that knowledge, you should be able to create your own unique dishes every day of your life.

Pino Luongo
New York City
October 2003

how to use this book

This book is organized a bit differently from most cookbooks.

First of all, the recipe chapters are arranged by key ingredient. There's a chapter on bread, a chapter on mushrooms, a chapter on fish and shellfish, and so on. Within each chapter, recipes are organized as much as possible by the order in which you would encounter them in an Italian meal: appetizer (which I use to mean hors d'oeuvre, small starter, or the first of two courses preceding a more substantial main-course dish), salad, soup, pasta, and main course. I say "as much as possible" because many of the recipes can be used for more than one purpose. A pasta, for instance, can be an appetizer, pasta course (which in an Italian meal would come between the antipasto, or hors d'oeuvre, and the main course), or in some cases a main course. In these incidents, I've organized the recipes according to the first place they *might* be used in a meal.

Two notes on exceptions to this structure: occasionally, I've indicated that a recipe can be used as a side dish, to accompany a main course, and in a very few cases I specify *brunch* main course because that's the only time I'd serve it. The last chapter, which focuses on cheese and dessert, is organized first by cheese and then by sweets.

Second, each recipe has two headnotes, Il Classico (The Classic) and La Mia Versione (My Version). The former explains the classic Tuscan, Italian, or American idea that inspired the recipe, and the latter explains how we've altered it to create something new.

The recipes are supported by three recurring features:

How to Prepare and Enjoy . . .
This is where I'll explain certain ingredients and techniques, such as how to store fresh pasta or how to shuck an oyster or clean littleneck clams.

In Search of . . .

This is where I'll describe traditional Italian ingredients such as pancetta, dried porcini mushrooms, and vin santo and, where appropriate, offer American substitutions.

Vino

I enjoy wine with just about every meal. This is where I'll share my thoughts on what type of wine you should select to go with each dish. In keeping with the theme of the book, I have not confined myself to Italian wines.

A Note About Photographs

In the spirit of this book, we gave our photographer, Michele Tabozzi, free rein in visually interpreting the recipes. In some instances, you will notice differences between the ingredients and plating style in the written recipe and those in the photograph of the dish. In all cases, the written version is the one that should be followed.

PANE
BREAD

A Tuscan baby cries. He's hungry. So he cries. He shrieks. He screams. Then something finds its way into his mouth. Initially hard and dry, it grows soft and moist as he sucks on it. It feels good, and, though he hasn't swallowed a thing, his appetite is sated. He stops crying and focuses his full attention on the pleasure being unleashed on his new, rapidly developing palate.

Our little friend has just had his first taste of pane, or bread, a piece of crust that his parents have given him as a pacifier.

Tuscans get to know bread at the same time we get to know our own families, like this little boy sucking on his first crust. In a few months he will enjoy the most enviable baby foods in the world, panelatte (bread cubes soaked in warm milk and tossed with sugar, cinnamon, or powdered chocolate) and pappa al pomodoro (tomato and bread soup).

When he becomes a teenager, he will discover more sophisticated pleasures, like a thick slice of country toast, lightly charred where it met the hot grates of a grill and spread with cool, creamy ricotta cheese as an accompaniment to his morning cappuccino. As an adult he will be eating dinner one night and realize that, as part of his maturation, bread has become his third hand, used to push food onto forks or soak up the last little puddle of soup in a bowl or the oily tomato sauce that clings to a plate after the pasta is gone.

There are hundreds of varieties of bread throughout Italy, and the people of each region are very particular about theirs. In the South, where Tuscany is situated, peasant bread with a hefty dough and hard crust is the favorite. Most households bake theirs once a week, use it until it grows stale, then—in a miracle of pragmatism—resurrect it in soups and salads, where it absorbs broths and tangy, acidic dressings.

Pasta gets more attention around the world, but to a Tuscan bread is just as important. Perhaps even more important. We love bread so much that, despite what the history books say, I like to think that we originally invented olive oil as a condiment for bread alone. Those two Tuscan staples are, when you stop to think about it, one of the most perfect dialogues between mankind and nature in all of gastronomy.

CROUTON

IL CLASSICO

A crostino is a slice of Tuscan bread spread with a topping such as chicken liver pâté or pureed white beans. In most countries a crouton is a supporting element, something to be floated in a soup or served alongside a salad. While a crostino can also be used for this purpose, it is most likely to be employed as a stand-alone hors d'oeuvre when you sit down to a meal at a home or in a restaurant.

LA MIA VERSIONE 1

CROSTINI DI CAVOLO NERO CON PANCETTA

BLACK CABBAGE AND BACON CROUTON

SERVES 4 AS AN APPETIZER

Black cabbage is one of the classic crostini toppings, especially as a counterpoint to the freshest olive oil, which is available just after the November press. This first press, or cold press, harks back to ancient times, when hand-picking and stone-mashing kept the oil cool throughout production, maintaining its character and reflecting the personality of the land, geography, and soil from which it hailed. This recipe makes one major adjustment to the original: the addition of bacon. (We use American bacon here in place of the Italian pancetta; it works just as well in this context and is easier to find.)

COARSE SALT

6 BLACK CABBAGE LEAVES

3 TABLESPOONS EXTRA VIRGIN OLIVE OIL

1 SMALL ONION, ROUGHLY CHOPPED

2 TABLESPOONS MINCED BACON

FRESHLY GROUND BLACK PEPPER

FOUR ½-INCH-THICK SLICES TUSCAN COUNTRY BREAD

1 Bring a small pot of lightly salted water to a boil. Cook the black cabbage leaves in the water for 5 minutes, then strain through a fine-mesh strainer set over a bowl. Set aside the cabbage leaves and cooking liquid separately.

2 Heat 2 tablespoons of the olive oil in a sauté pan over medium-high heat. Add the onion and bacon and cook until both are browned, 4 to 5 minutes. Add the cabbage and 2 tablespoons of the reserved cooking liquid. Season with black pepper and sauté for 2 minutes. (The mixture should be juicy; if it appears dry, add some more reserved cooking liquid.) Set the pan aside, covered, to keep the mixture warm.

(continued)

3 Toast the bread. If serving as an hors d'oeuvre, cut the slices in half. Divide the cabbage leaf–bacon mixture among the slices. Drizzle with the remaining olive oil and season with a few grinds of black pepper. Serve at once, either on small plates or from a platter.

IN SEARCH OF . . . CAVOLO NERO
Cavolo nero, or black cabbage, is very difficult to find in the United States, although it is grown in the Boston area. It is very similar to kale and can be replaced in this and other recipes with an equal quantity of kale, Swiss chard, or broccoli di rapa (broccoli rabe) leaves.

VINO Serve this with a full-bodied Chianti Reserve from Tuscany that is at least three years old.

LA MIA VERSIONE 2

CROSTINI DI ACCIUGHE E MOZZARELLA
ANCHOVY AND MOZZARELLA CROUTON

———

SERVES 6 AS AN APPETIZER

The ingredients for this recipe mirror those in another classic crostino, which stacks an anchovy fillet and a slice of mozzarella atop the bread. The difference here is in the preparation, which allows you to make all the crostini at once, baking the bread in loaf form and then separating the slices just before serving.

6 SMALL BAGUETTES

¾ POUND MOZZARELLA, CUT INTO ½-INCH-THICK SLICES

2 TABLESPOONS UNSALTED BUTTER

12 ANCHOVY FILLETS PACKED IN OLIVE OIL, UNRINSED

12 TO 18 CAPER BERRIES

1 Preheat the oven to 300°F.

2 Slice the baguettes crosswise at 1-inch intervals, being careful not to cut all the way through. Place slices of mozzarella in the spaces between the bread slices.

3 Place the baguettes on a rimmed cookie sheet without crowding and bake until the cheese is melted and the bread crispy, 8 to 10 minutes.

4 Meanwhile, melt the butter in a small sauté pan over medium-high heat and, with the help of a wooden spoon, dissolve the anchovies in it.

5 Separate the slices of each baguette and arrange them on a platter. Pour some foaming anchovy-butter mixture over the crostini. Garnish with caper berries. Serve at once.

VINO Serve this with the youngest Vermentino that you can find from Cinque Terre, Liguria.

LA MIA VERSIONE 3

CROSTINI D'ACQUACOTTA

COUNTRY BREAD WITH TOMATO-MUSHROOM STEW

SERVES 6 AS AN APPETIZER

This recipe uses the same ingredients you might find in a traditional acquacotta but varies the proportions to create a crostino. Reducing the amount of liquid in the "soup" makes it thick and spreadable. This recipe references the regional variation of acquacotta made in Maremma, where an egg is poached in the soup. We did not choose a quail egg here to be trendy; a chicken egg is simply too big to fit atop a crostino.

Incidentally, acquacotta is a zuppa di pane (bread soup), one of a family of Italian soups in which bread plays a central role. The most celebrated example is pappa al pomodoro (page 11), where bread is one of two primary ingredients. But often a zuppa di pane is simply a soup spooned over a slice of toasted country bread placed in the bottom of the bowl just before serving, as with a cacciucco, a soup made with olive oil, garlic, rockfish, and other ingredients.

1 Wipe the mushrooms clean with a damp towel. Remove and discard the stems and slice the caps ¼ inch thick. (If using porcini, keep the stems; peel them with a paring knife and remove any spoiled part, then slice them to the same size as the caps.)

2 Heat 2 tablespoons of the olive oil in a sauté pan over medium heat. Add the garlic and cook until lightly browned, about 3 minutes. Add the mushrooms, stir, season with salt and pepper, and cook over medium heat for 3 to 4 minutes. Add the tomatoes and cook until wilted, about 30 seconds. Add the vegetable stock, give the mixture a good stir, and cook for 5 minutes or until the mixture is fairly dry but still a bit moist.

(continued)

1½ POUNDS WILD MUSHROOMS, IDEALLY FRESH PORCINI OR MORELS

¼ CUP EXTRA VIRGIN OLIVE OIL

4 GARLIC CLOVES, CRUSHED AND PEELED

FINE SEA SALT

FRESHLY GROUND BLACK PEPPER

12 RIPE CHERRY TOMATOES, HALVED

½ CUP VEGETABLE STOCK

FEW DROPS WHITE VINEGAR

12 QUAIL EGGS

6 SLICES TUSCAN COUNTRY BREAD, TOASTED

3 Meanwhile, bring a small pot of water to a boil. Add a few drops of white vinegar. One by one, crack the quail eggs into a tablespoon and lower them into the water. Let them poach for 1 minute, then remove with a slotted spoon and gather them on a plate.

4 Arrange the warm croutons on a platter. Spoon some acquacotta (mushroom-tomato mixture) over each one and place 2 quail eggs on each. Drizzle with the remaining olive oil. Serve at once.

VINO A full-bodied Australian Shiraz is a big, bold match for the rich quail egg in this recipe.

PIZZA SOUFFLÉ

—

SERVES 6 AS AN APPETIZER

IL CLASSICO

Sformato is a catchall Italian word referring to recipes that use an egg as a binding element to hold other ingredients together. The result can resemble a soufflé or custard.

LA MIA VERSIONE

This is a dish that my corporate chef Marta's mother made for her when she was growing up in Rome. Unlike more traditional sformato, this resembles bread pudding.

Serve this with a green salad for a simple lunch.

⅓ CUP EXTRA VIRGIN OLIVE OIL

2 GARLIC CLOVES, THINLY SLICED

ONE AND A HALF 14½-OUNCE CANS CRUSHED TOMATOES

10 FRESH BASIL LEAVES, TORN BY HAND

COARSE SALT

FRESHLY GROUND BLACK PEPPER

2 CUPS WHOLE MILK

¾ POUND DENSE WHITE SANDWICH BREAD, SLICED ¼ INCH THICK

¾ POUND MOZZARELLA, SLICED ¼ INCH THICK

1 CUP GRATED PARMIGIANO-REGGIANO

3 TEASPOONS DRIED OREGANO

3 LARGE EGGS

1 Preheat the oven to 350°F.

2 Warm 3 tablespoons of the olive oil in a deep wide sauté pan over medium heat. Add the garlic and sauté until brown, 3 to 5 minutes. Add the tomatoes and about 4 torn basil leaves, season with salt and pepper, stir, and cook for 15 minutes. Remove from the heat and set aside to cool.

3 Pour the remaining olive oil into a baking pan about 11 x 7 x 3 inches.

4 Pour the milk into a wide, shallow vessel and soak the bread slices in the milk, one at a time, for 1 second each. Layer enough bread slices in the bottom of the pan to cover in a single layer. Arrange a layer of mozzarella on top. Sprinkle with grated Parmigiano, oregano, and basil and cover with a thin layer of tomato sauce. Arrange 2 more layers in the same way.

5 Break the eggs into the bowl with the remaining milk. Add the remaining Parmigiano, season with pepper, and beat with a whisk until fluffy.

6 Pour the mixture over the contents of the baking pan and bake until risen and golden brown, about 50 minutes. Cut into individual portions and serve hot.

VINO The light and delicious flavor of a young Frascati from the outskirts of Rome complements the fluffy texture of this dish.

PAPPA DI POLENTA AL POMODORO

CORNMEAL AND TOMATO SOUP

———

SERVES 6 AS AN APPETIZER OR A SOUP

IL CLASSICO

Pappa al pomodoro is simple, humble, and ingenious. Fashioned from a handful of Tuscan staples, it is texturally very complex—a pleasingly primordial soup in which liquefied tomato pulp (the name of the dish actually means "tomato pap"), bread, and stock become an indistinguishable whole.

In the United States, much is made of this quintessential Tuscan soup: because the recipe actually calls for stale bread, it demonstrates the resourcefulness of the Tuscan kitchen. This is true: pappa al pomodoro is one of the most Renaissance dishes there is—every mouthful delivers taste and fulfillment highlighted by a natural saltiness and the poetry of fresh herbs.

But pappa al pomodoro exemplifies another defining aspect of Tuscan cooking as well: profound love for the harmony that can naturally exist between two ingredients. Our cuisine brims with such duos, from bread and tomatoes to fava beans and Pecorino Toscano to prosciutto di Parma and Parmigiano-Reggiano. Understanding the logic behind these perfect pairings is the gateway to fully appreciating (and successfully cooking) our deceptively simple recipes.

LA MIA VERSIONE

Polenta is one of the most adaptable Tuscan recipes. Its absorbency allows the cook to vary the liquid (water, stock, milk, cream, or a combination) and then pair the cooked polenta with almost anything. In this recipe we simply replace pappa al pomodoro's bread with polenta, creating a more complex soup that, to American diners, might seem vaguely southwestern. Be sure that the tomatoes are completely broken down before adding the polenta, or the cornmeal will soak up only the broth, leaving the tomato chunks intact.

(continued)

½ CUP EXTRA VIRGIN OLIVE OIL

1 SMALL ONION, ROUGHLY CHOPPED

1 GARLIC CLOVE, MINCED

TWO 14½-OUNCE CANS DICED TOMATOES

**14 FRESH BASIL LEAVES,
8 OF THEM TORN BY HAND**

FINE SEA SALT

FRESHLY GROUND BLACK PEPPER

**2 QUARTS VEGETABLE STOCK, SIMMERING IN A
POT ON A BACK BURNER**

1½ CUPS QUICK-COOKING POLENTA

½ CUP GRATED PARMIGIANO-REGGIANO

PAPPA AL POMODORO...
WITH FISH
Pappa al pomodoro is so thick that
it could be served on a plate rather
than in a bowl, and I recommend
doing just that for another
application. Cook the soup until it
is reduced and can be spooned
onto a plate, then use it as an
accompaniment for roasted sea
bass, halibut, or cod. After plating
the dish, spoon any remaining
liquid from the pappa over and
around the fish as a sauce. You can
also use pappa al pomodoro as a
side dish with other hearty dishes.
After fish, my next choice would be
a grilled Florentine steak (see
headnotes on pages 51 and 208).

1 In a 3- to 5-quart pot, warm ¼ cup of the olive oil over medium-high heat. Add the onion and garlic and sauté until golden brown, about 5 minutes.

2 Add the tomatoes and 4 torn basil leaves, season with salt and pepper, and cook for 10 minutes.

3 Add 6 cups of the simmering vegetable stock and 4 more torn basil leaves. Raise the heat to high, bring the stock to a boil, then lower the heat and simmer for 20 minutes. Taste and add salt and pepper if necessary.

4 Slowly add the polenta while whisking and keep whisking until it becomes thick enough to slow the whisk as you work it. (If the polenta becomes too thick, resembling a solid more than a porridge, whisk in more simmering stock as needed.)

5 Remove the pot from the stove and divide the soup among 6 bowls. Finish each with a drizzle of the remaining olive oil, a few grinds of black pepper, and a sprinkling of Parmigiano. Rest a basil leaf on top of the soup in the center of each bowl and serve at once.

IN SEARCH OF . . . EXTRA VIRGIN OLIVE OIL
To taste all the nuances of pappa al pomodoro, drizzle some high-quality, first-press, extra virgin olive oil over it. The oil will be the perfect foil for the tomato and the bread—a powerful illustration of the natural chemistry of Tuscan cuisine.

VINO I'm torn between two wines here. One great choice would be the youngest Tuscan Vernaccia you can get your hands on, with lots of green-apple flavor. Another, equally appealing option is a very dry, slightly smoky Sauvignon from the Veneto or Friuli.

TWICE-BOILED-SOUP RAVIOLI WITH BLACK CABBAGE AND BACON

———

SERVES 6 AS AN APPETIZER OR 4 AS A MAIN COURSE

IL CLASSICO

Ribollita, perhaps the quintessential Florentine soup, means "reboiled." You make the soup the day before you plan to eat it, then, when you reheat it, the vegetables and bread break down to create a thick soup that's hearty enough to be a meal on its own.

LA MIA VERSIONE

This recipe takes advantage of ribollita's thickness, using it as a ravioli filling. Aficionados of white-bean ravioli will love this, because the flavor and texture of the cannellini beans predominate.

½ CUP EXTRA VIRGIN OLIVE OIL

1 CUP MINCED CELERY

1 CUP MINCED CARROT

1 CUP MINCED ONION

2 CUPS PEELED YUKON GOLD POTATO IN ¼-INCH DICE

FINE SEA SALT

1½ CUPS DRIED CANNELLINI BEANS, SOAKED OVERNIGHT OR FOR AT LEAST 6 HOURS IN COLD WATER TO COVER

3 CUPS TIGHTLY PACKED BLACK CABBAGE LEAVES CUT INTO ½-INCH STRIPS (SEE IN SEARCH OF . . . , PAGE 6)

6 CUPS VEGETABLE STOCK, SIMMERING IN A POT ON A BACK BURNER

2 CUPS CRUSTLESS TUSCAN COUNTRY BREAD IN 1-INCH CUBES, DRIED IN A 250°F OVEN FOR 15 MINUTES

2 TABLESPOONS FRESH THYME LEAVES

¼ CUP FRESHLY GRATED PARMIGIANO-REGGIANO

FRESHLY GROUND BLACK PEPPER

RIBOLLITA FILLING

1 Pour half the olive oil into a 4-quart flameproof casserole and tilt the casserole to let the oil coat the bottom. Warm over medium heat, then add the celery, carrot, and onion and sauté for 15 minutes. Add the potato, stir, season with 2 teaspoons salt, and cook for another 5 minutes.

2 Drain the soaked beans and add them along with the black cabbage and 1 quart of the hot vegetable stock. Season with another 2 teaspoons salt. Simmer for 40 minutes or until the beans are soft, adding a little more stock whenever the soup gets dry. Add the bread, stirring it thoroughly into the mixture, then remove the pot from the stove and finish the soup with the thyme, Parmigiano, and remaining olive oil. Taste and adjust the seasoning with black pepper and, if necessary, more salt. The soup should be very thick. Allow it to cool at room temperature while you make the pasta.

(continued)

6 CUPS DURUM FLOUR OR ALL-PURPOSE FLOUR, PLUS MORE FOR DUSTING WORK SURFACE

7 LARGE EGGS, BEATEN

1 On a clean, floured work surface, mound the flour and make a well in the center.

2 Slowly pour the eggs into the well and work the flour into the center with a fork until the eggs are absorbed. Knead by hand until the dough has a smooth and even consistency. Divide the pasta dough into 4 pieces and wrap them individually in plastic wrap to keep them from drying out.

3 Make thin pasta sheets by passing each portion of dough repeatedly through a pasta machine or rolling it with a rolling pin, until about ⅛ inch thick. Set aside.

IN SEARCH OF . . . DURUM FLOUR

The term *durum flour* means "hard flour." Also known as "00" flour, this Italian favorite is available from Italian grocers and specialty shops.

1 LARGE EGG YOLK, LIGHTLY BEATEN

FINE SEA SALT

¼ CUP EXTRA VIRGIN OLIVE OIL

2 CUPS SLAB BACON IN ¼-INCH DICE

3 CUPS TIGHTLY PACKED BLACK CABBAGE LEAVES, STEAMED UNTIL TENDER AND CUT INTO 1-INCH STRIPS

½ CUP GRATED PARMIGIANO-REGGIANO

RAVIOLI, SAUCE, AND ASSEMBLY

1 Place heaping teaspoons of soup on a pasta sheet, 1 inch apart, leaving a border of 1 inch on all sides.

2 Make an egg wash by mixing the egg yolk with ¼ cup water. Brush the pasta sheet around the mounds of filling. Lay another sheet over the mounds, letting it conform to the shapes. Cut the ravioli into squares with a rolling cutter, seal the edges with the tines of a fork, and place them on a floured tray. Repeat with the remaining pasta and filling.

3 Bring a large pot of salted water to a boil over high heat.

4 Heat 2 tablespoons of the olive oil in a sauté pan over medium heat. Add the bacon and cook until crispy, about 7 minutes, then add the black cabbage and sauté slowly, until it gets very soft, about 5 minutes. If necessary, add a few tablespoons of vegetable stock or water to keep it from drying out.

5 Add the ravioli to the boiling water and cook until they float to the surface, 1 to 2 minutes. Use a slotted spoon to transfer them to a serving platter. Drizzle with the remaining olive oil, spoon the bacon-cabbage sauce over them, and top with the grated Parmigiano. Serve at once.

IN SEARCH OF . . . PANCETTA

Often nicknamed "Italian bacon," pancetta is much more than the Italian version of the prepackaged bacon we associate with supermarkets here in the United States. Pancetta is cured pork cut from the belly of the pig and is usually seasoned with pepper and cloves. It is one of the most popular ingredients in Italian cooking because using it in the base of a dish infuses the other ingredients with rich and aromatic flavor.

VINO Serve this with a very-full-bodied Merlot from Australia.

LASAGNE OF BREAD AND CAULIFLOWER

——

SERVES 6 AS AN APPETIZER OR 4 AS A MAIN COURSE

IL CLASSICO

Everybody knows lasagne: it's one of the few Italian dishes to make it to American shores intact, still looking and tasting like it did back home. The most famous variation is lasagne Bolognese, with a tangy red meat sauce.

LA MIA VERSIONE

Years ago at one of my first restaurants, Le Madri, we created a sensation with our focaccia robiola, a "white pizza" made by halving a round of focaccia horizontally, filling it with creamy Robiola cheese, baking it, and drizzling it with white truffle oil. It has become one of the most imitated pizzas in New York. This recipe is fashioned in a similar spirit, taking bread and cauliflower soup and making it the basis of a "white lasagne" by using slices of day-old bread dipped in cauliflower florets' cooking liquid. Pecorino Toscano and black pepper add body and flavor. Be careful not to oversalt the cauliflower cooking liquid.

FINE SEA SALT

2 POUNDS CAULIFLOWER, THICK STALKS DISCARDED, SEPARATED INTO FLORETS

¼ CUP PLUS 2 TABLESPOONS EXTRA VIRGIN OLIVE OIL

ONE ¾-POUND LOAF TUSCAN COUNTRY BREAD, ENDS TRIMMED AND DISCARDED, SLICED CROSSWISE ½ INCH THICK AND TOASTED

10 OUNCES 3- TO 6-MONTH-OLD PECORINO TOSCANO, GRATED

FRESHLY GROUND BLACK PEPPER

1 Preheat the oven to 325°F.

2 Fill a medium pot with water and add 2 tablespoons salt. Bring to a boil over high heat. Add the cauliflower and cook until soft, 4 to 6 minutes. Strain the cauliflower liquid through a fine-mesh strainer placed over a bowl. Set aside the florets and the cooking liquid.

3 Pour ¼ cup of the olive oil into a baking pan measuring about 11 inches x 8 inches, tipping the pan from side to side and using your fingers to coat the bottom and sides evenly.

4 Lightly soak half the toasted bread slices a few at a time in the cauliflower cooking liquid and arrange in a single layer on the bottom of the baking pan. Sprinkle half the cauliflower evenly over the bread, top with half the Pecorino, season generously with black pepper, and drizzle with 1 tablespoon of the remaining olive oil. Add another

layer of bread, top with the remaining cauliflower and cheese, again season generously with black pepper, and drizzle on the remaining olive oil.

5 Cover with foil and bake for 10 minutes. Remove the foil and continue to bake for 20 minutes or until golden on top. Cut into portions and serve at once.

VINO Morellino di Scansano, from southern Tuscany, is an underappreciated wine worth discovering, especially with this unique rustic dish.

ROASTED TOMATO AND PESTO SANDWICH

SERVES 4 AS AN APPETIZER OR 8 AS A SIDE DISH

IL CLASSICO

The greatest thing my mother ever made for me was the simplest, which forever shaped my philosophy of cooking. She rubbed tomatoes on slices of bread, then chilled the bread in the refrigerator until it was soft and cool. Most people will tell you never to refrigerate tomatoes, but this is one case where it's absolutely the right thing to do. I also love the classic bruschetta—diced tomatoes and thin slivers of basil on a slice of garlic-rubbed toast.

LA MIA VERSIONE

This recipe takes the ingredients of a bruschetta and makes them into a sandwich. The bread is toasted; plum tomatoes are sliced, tossed with olive oil and minced garlic, and roasted; and the basil is represented by pesto. If you make and store pesto in the summer, you can enjoy this sandwich all year long. This is also a wonderful accompaniment to fish dishes in place of bread on the side.

1½ POUNDS FIRM VINE-RIPENED TOMATOES, SLICED ½ INCH THICK

2 TEASPOONS COARSE SALT

½ TEASPOON SUGAR

4 GARLIC CLOVES, MINCED

12 FRESH BASIL LEAVES, TORN BY HAND

½ TEASPOON FRESH THYME LEAVES

ROASTED TOMATOES

1 Preheat the oven to 300°F and keep the door slightly ajar with a cork or other flameproof item to help circulate the air.

2 Line a rimmed cookie sheet with parchment paper and arrange the tomato slices on it in a single layer. Mix the salt and sugar together in a small bowl and sprinkle the tomatoes with the mixture. Then sprinkle with the garlic, basil, and thyme.

3 Place the cookie sheet in the oven and bake for 90 minutes, until the tomatoes are dried but not shriveled. Meanwhile, make the pesto.

PESTO

1 Place the basil, pine nuts, garlic, olive oil, 2 tablespoons cool water, and 1 large ice cube in a blender and pulse until a thick mixture is formed. (The ice cube will keep the heat of the blade from cooking and discoloring the basil.)

2 Transfer the mixture to a bowl, stir in the Parmigiano and Pecorino, taste, and, if necessary, add salt. (The cheeses may be salty enough that no additional seasoning is necessary.)

60 FRESH BASIL LEAVES

1½ TABLESPOONS PINE NUTS

1 GARLIC CLOVE, PEELED AND SMASHED

¼ CUP EXTRA VIRGIN OLIVE OIL

1½ TABLESPOONS GRATED PARMIGIANO-REGGIANO

1½ TABLESPOONS GRATED PECORINO ROMANO

COARSE SALT

ASSEMBLY

1 Toast or grill the bread slices.

2 Place 4 slices on a serving tray and arrange the tomatoes on top. Drizzle with the pesto, cover with the remaining bread slices, and cut into quarters. Serve warm.

VINO A Zinfandel from Oregon provides a great contrast to this very humble dish.

8 SLICES TUSCAN COUNTRY BREAD

CEREALI
GRAINS AND LEGUMES

It seems
that the people of every country have unflattering, often offensive nicknames for the people of certain other lands or even snobby, hurtful ways of referring to those from other parts of their own nation. Italians who live far to the north or south of Florence have one derogatory nickname for Tuscans. It is *mangiafagioli,* which means "bean eaters."

Well, let me tell you something, my friend. There are a lot of names you better not call me. But feel free to call me a mangiafagioli any day, because I take it as a compliment. The negative connotation of the word is that we Tuscans are a poor people who have no choice but to sustain ourselves on a diet of readily available, inexpensive beans. But the positive interpretation is that we are persistent, creative, and revolutionary with these ingredients. In fact I think of us as *mago-dei-fagioli,* or "bean magicians," because we spin beans into culinary gold, just as we do other legumes and the diverse family of grains. I find poetic justice in the fact that grains and legumes (collectively known as *cereali* in Tuscany) are fundamental to *cucina contadina* (peasant cuisine) because these ingredients are as resilient as the Tuscan people themselves.

Many of these foods have been around for centuries. Farro, or spelt, has been known to us since the Etruscan period, when it was ground into flour for bread or used in soups as a thickening agent. I like to replace the rice in risotto with spelt to make a farrotto because the hearty grain maintains its character in the finished dish rather than simply becoming a backdrop for the others. (In all honesty, I seem to be alone in this position; though Tuscany produces very little rice, risotto is so popular that you can find regional versions of it all over the area.) For the following recipes, seek out the grains sold as "farro," but if you can't find them use the American product sold as spelt.

Lentils have also been a mainstay of our diet for generations, dating all the way back to the days of the Medici. Personally, I enjoy experimenting by marrying them with other beans in recipes, like in a soup we serve at one of my restaurants that finds white beans, chickpeas, borlotti beans, and lentils coexisting peacefully.

If you ever have a chance to visit Tuscany in the summertime and have access to a kitchen, I encourage you to buy fresh beans and sample for yourself the wide variety produced by the different soil in each area. The differences are as profound as those conjured by the different terroirs in winegrowing regions. The beans are so impressive that a dish as elemental as fagioli al fiasco, beans simmered in a thick wine flask set over open coals, has become a Florentine classic.

But my fondest memories are of the wondrous tricks the mago-dei-fagioli work with chickpeas. In hindsight it feels as though I enjoyed a cecina fashioned from farina di ceci (chickpea flour), water, oil, and rosemary every single day of my childhood. It amazes me that today, in southeastern Tuscany, little out-of-the-way trattorias still make this dish. Many of them will sell you one through a window, allowing you to stroll without pause along the ancient streets eating this ancient product of the mago-dei-fagioli and savoring all the humble history it brings so effortlessly to mind.

LENTILS

IL CLASSICO

Italians are open, lenient people, but we do have a number of culinary rules that are strict, even if they are unspoken. Lentils, for example, are usually served in a thick brown soup or simmered in stock or water with diced sweet vegetables like celery and carrot and served as a salad or side dish, most famously with the pork sausage we call *cotechino*.

LA MIA VERSIONE 1

INSALATA TIEPIDA DI LENTICCHIE E CAPESANTE

WARM LENTIL AND SCALLOP SALAD

SERVES 4 AS AN APPETIZER

In recent years lentils have been found to have an affinity for fish and shellfish, as in this recipe, which matches them with scallops.

---

1 CUP DRIED LENTILS

FINE SEA SALT

1 SMALL ONION, PEELED

1 BAY LEAF

PINCH OF GROUND CUMIN

3 CUPS VEGETABLE STOCK

FRESHLY GROUND BLACK PEPPER

16 LARGE SEA SCALLOPS

½ CUP EXTRA VIRGIN OLIVE OIL

1 FRESH ROSEMARY SPRIG

12 CHERRY TOMATOES, BLANCHED AND PEELED (SEE NOTE)

1 Place the lentils in a small pot and add cold water to cover. Lightly salt the water. Add the whole onion, bay leaf, and cumin and bring to a boil over high heat, then lower the heat and simmer until the lentils are cooked but still al dente, about 20 minutes. Remove from the heat and let the lentils cool in their cooking liquid.

2 In a deep wide pan, bring the vegetable stock to a simmer over moderate heat. Season with salt and pepper and carefully lower the scallops into the liquid without crowding. (You may need to do this in 2 batches.) Poach the scallops until they are firm to the touch, 4 to 5 minutes, then remove them to a plate and cover them to keep them warm.

3 Warm half the olive oil in a small flameproof casserole over medium-high heat. Add the rosemary. When the oil is hot but not yet bubbling, add the cherry tomatoes and gently sauté them in the oil for 5 minutes.

4 Use tongs to pick out and discard the bay leaf and onion from the pot with the lentils. Pour off most of the cooking liquid, but leave the lentils just the slightest bit soupy. Divide them among 4 large bowls and arrange 4 scallops and 3 tomatoes over each portion. Finish with a drizzle of olive oil and a few grinds of black pepper. Serve at once.

VINO I like to serve red wine with scallops, especially if there are lentils on the plate. Select a young Pinot Noir from Oregon.

PEELING TOMATOES
To peel tomatoes, remove the stem and cut a shallow X in the tomato's skin at the bottom of the fruit. Bring a pot of water to a boil and lower the tomatoes into the water. After 20 to 30 seconds, remove the tomatoes with a slotted spoon and transfer them to a bowl filled with ice water. As soon as the tomatoes are cool enough to handle, peel the skin off, using a paring knife if necessary.

HERBED TOMATO OIL
After the tomatoes are removed from their cooking oil, the oil—which will be infused with the flavor of the tomatoes and rosemary—can be cooled and saved for another use. You might, for example, use it as the basis for a summery vinaigrette.

LA MIA VERSIONE 2

FUSILLI CON LENTICCHIE, GAMBERI, E PANCETTA
SPIRAL PASTA WITH LENTILS, SHRIMP, AND BACON

SERVES 6 AS AN APPETIZER OR 4 AS A MAIN COURSE

White beans are often used in Tuscan pasta sauces (as well as in the classic pasta and bean soup), but lentils are reserved mostly for minestre, or Tuscan soups featuring pasta. It turns out they are a natural and sometimes preferable alternative to their pale cousins in pasta sauces, as in this recipe, where their earthy flavor is a better foil for the pasta, shrimp, and bacon than any white bean.

(continued)

¼ CUP DRIED LENTILS

2 SMALL ONIONS, PEELED, 1 QUARTERED BUT
LEFT ATTACHED BY THE ROOT END, 1 ROUGHLY
CHOPPED

1 SMALL CARROT, PEELED

2 BAY LEAVES

FINE SEA SALT

¼ CUP PLUS 2 TABLESPOONS EXTRA VIRGIN
OLIVE OIL

3 OUNCES SLAB BACON, CUT INTO SMALL DICE

8 LARGE SHRIMP, SHELLED AND DEVEINED

¼ CUP DRY WHITE WINE

FRESHLY GROUND BLACK PEPPER

1 POUND FUSILLI

1 Put the lentils in a small pot. Add the quartered onion, carrot, and bay leaves and cover with cold water by 1 inch. Place over high heat and bring the water to a boil. Lower the heat and simmer until the lentils are cooked but still al dente, 25 to 30 minutes. Remove from the heat and let the lentils cool in the cooking liquid.

2 While the lentils are cooling, bring a large pot of salted water to a boil over high heat.

3 Meanwhile, pour 2 tablespoons of the olive oil into a sauté pan and set over medium-high heat. Add the bacon and chopped onion and cook until some fat is rendered from the bacon, 2 to 3 minutes. Add the shrimp and sauté for 2 minutes. Pour the wine over the shrimp and cook until it evaporates, about 1 minute.

4 Drain the cooled lentils in a colander set over a bowl, setting aside the cooking liquid and lentils separately. Use tongs to pick out and discard the onion quarters, carrot, and bay leaf. Add the drained lentils and ½ cup of the reserved cooking liquid to the pan with the shrimp and simmer for 2 to 3 minutes. Season to taste with salt and pepper.

5 Add the pasta to the pot of boiling water. Cook until al dente, about 10 minutes. Drain the pasta and add it to the sauce. Toss or stir well and finish with the remaining olive oil. If necessary, add some more cooking liquid from the lentils to keep the sauce loose and prevent the lentils from becoming too dry. Serve at once, either by dividing among individual bowls or family style from the center of the table.

VINO A sparkling Prosecco from the Veneto, with its hints of vanilla, offers refreshing contrast to the smoky flavor of the bacon in this dish.

SALAD OF SWEET CORN, PEAS, AND SPELT

———

SERVES 4 AS AN APPETIZER

IL CLASSICO

Panzanella is a bread salad that Tuscans enjoy in the summertime. It's traditionally made with day-old, slightly stale bread that is softened when tossed with a vinegary dressing, which is allowed to soak into it. It is sometimes also made with farro, or spelt, a beadlike grain. That variation is known as *panzanella di farro*.

LA MIA VERSIONE

This recipe is based on panzanella di farro but augments the grain with a variety of small ingredients that are at their peak of freshness in the early summer: sweet corn, cherry tomatoes, and sweet peas.

SALAD

FINE SEA SALT

¾ CUP SPELT, CLEANED IN SEVERAL CHANGES OF COLD WATER

1 CUP FRESH SWEET CORN KERNELS

½ CUP SCALLION, WHITE AND LIGHT GREEN PARTS, IN THIN DIAGONAL SLICES

16 RIPE CHERRY TOMATOES

1 CUP FRESH PEAS, BLANCHED

8 FRESH MINT LEAVES, TORN BY HAND

Bring a pot of salted water to a boil. Add the spelt and cook until al dente, 25 to 35 minutes. Drain and refresh it under cold running water. Transfer the spelt to a large bowl and add the other ingredients.

DRESSING AND ASSEMBLY

1 TEASPOON FINE SEA SALT

2 TABLESPOONS RED WINE VINEGAR

¼ CUP EXTRA VIRGIN OLIVE OIL

1 CUP LOOSELY PACKED ARUGULA

1 Put the salt in a small bowl and dissolve it in the vinegar by mixing with a whisk. Add the olive oil in a thin stream, whisking to form an emulsified dressing.

2 Pour the dressing over the salad and toss gently. Divide the arugula among 4 salad plates and divide the salad among the plates. Serve at once.

VINO Serve this with a crisp, clean, young Riesling from Trentino Alto-Adige.

WHITE BEAN, WATERCRESS, AND BLOOD ORANGE SALAD

SERVES 4 TO 6 AS AN APPETIZER OR 8 AS A SIDE DISH

IL CLASSICO

The tart flavor of blood orange (or, indeed, any variety of orange) is a perennial and versatile favorite, not just in Tuscany but throughout the Mediterranean, where it is often paired with fennel.

LA MIA VERSIONE

This recipe finds new companions for blood oranges, namely cannellini beans, watercress, and lemon juice. Serve this with any roasted white-fleshed fish.

---

2 CUPS DRIED CANNELLINI BEANS, SOAKED OVERNIGHT OR FOR AT LEAST 6 HOURS IN COLD WATER TO COVER

1 SMALL ONION, PEELED

1 FRESH SAGE SPRIG

1 GARLIC CLOVE, PEELED AND SMASHED

FINE SEA SALT

JUICE OF ½ BLOOD ORANGE

JUICE OF ½ LEMON

¼ CUP PLUS 1 TABLESPOON EXTRA VIRGIN OLIVE OIL

8 SCALLIONS, WHITE PARTS ONLY, DIAGONALLY SLICED ¼ INCH THICK

1 BLOOD ORANGE, PEELED AND DIVIDED INTO SEGMENTS

LEAVES FROM 2 BUNCHES WATERCRESS, RINSED AND SPUN DRY

FRESHLY GROUND BLACK PEPPER

1 Drain the cannellini beans and transfer them to a pot with the whole onion, sage, and garlic. Cover with cold water, season lightly with salt, and bring to a boil over high heat. Lower the heat and simmer until cooked but still al dente, about 45 minutes. Remove the pot from the heat and let the beans cool in their cooking liquid. (If the beans seem soft after soaking, cook them in a wider pot; they will cook more quickly if spread out.)

2 Pour the blood orange juice and lemon juice into a small bowl and add ½ teaspoon salt. Whisk until the salt is dissolved. Continue to whisk, adding the olive oil gradually in a thin stream, until an emulsified dressing is formed.

3 Drain the beans in a colander and use tongs to pick out and discard the onion, sage, and garlic. Transfer the beans to a salad bowl. Add the scallions, blood orange segments, and watercress leaves. Drizzle the vinaigrette over the salad, season with salt and pepper, and toss thoroughly but gently. Divide among individual plates and serve immediately or serve family style from the center of the table.

VINO This dish, reminiscent of southern Italian cuisine, screams for a good Sicilian wine. My favorite is Corvo Bianco.

OYSTER AND CHICKPEA SOUP

SERVES 4 TO 6 AS A SOUP

IL CLASSICO

In Tuscany we serve a very loose chickpea soup made with tubettini (a short, narrow tubular pasta) and clams, sort of a summery seaside version of pasta e fagioli.

LA MIA VERSIONE

The milky sweetness of chickpeas also complements oysters, which are poached gently in the soup during the final minutes of cooking.

1 In a medium flameproof casserole, sauté the bacon with 1 tablespoon of the olive oil over low heat until the bacon begins to render its fat, about 2 minutes. Raise the heat a bit, add the onion and garlic, and sauté until the onion is translucent, about 4 minutes. Add the potato, season with salt and pepper, then add the chickpeas and tarragon sprig. Stir well but gently and add enough hot water to cover the chickpeas by 3 inches. Raise the heat to high and bring the liquid to a boil. Lower the heat, cover, and simmer for 1 hour. (Add more hot water if the soup becomes too dry.)

2 When the hour is almost up, shuck the oysters, saving as much liquid as possible (see Note).

3 After the soup has been simmering for 1 hour, add the oysters and their liquid to the soup and cook for 5 more minutes. Remove the soup from the heat and finish with the remaining olive oil, the tarragon leaves, and a few grinds of black pepper. Divide among individual bowls and serve at once.

VINO Here's another dish that marries well with California Chardonnay.

HOW TO PREPARE AND ENJOY OYSTERS

To shuck an oyster, place a clean towel over one hand and take the oyster, cupped-side down, in that hand. (The towel is intended to protect you when shucking.) Take a small, sharp knife in your other hand and insert it into the oyster at the hinge. Carefully move the knife around inside the shell until the shell pops open. Open the shell and remove the oyster by cutting the muscle from the bottom shell with the knife. Reserve oysters in their liquid.

½ CUP BACON (ABOUT ¼ POUND) IN SMALL DICE

¼ CUP EXTRA VIRGIN OLIVE OIL

1 SMALL ONION, CHOPPED

1 GARLIC CLOVE, SLICED

1 MEDIUM IDAHO POTATO, PEELED AND CUT INTO ½-INCH DICE

FINE SEA SALT

FRESHLY GROUND BLACK PEPPER

1 CUP DRIED CHICKPEAS, SOAKED OVERNIGHT OR FOR AT LEAST 6 HOURS IN COLD WATER TO COVER AND DRAINED

1 FRESH TARRAGON SPRIG

AT LEAST 2 QUARTS WATER, SIMMERING IN A POT ON A BACK BURNER

24 OYSTERS, IDEALLY BELON OR GREYSTONE

1 TABLESPOON MINCED FRESH TARRAGON LEAVES

TUSCAN-STYLE CLAM CHOWDER

IL CLASSICO

As we all know, Manhattan clam chowder is a very simple, very brothy tomato soup. I've always loved it because it strikes me as an American dish with an Italian soul; in fact, some people have told me it's rumored to have been invented by Italian immigrants.

LA MIA VERSIONE

Although we have countless ways of serving clams in Tuscany, we have never come up with our own clam chowder . . . until now. This recipe "Tuscanizes" clam chowder with the addition of beans, barley, sage, and other shellfish.

FINE SEA SALT

½ CUP PEARL BARLEY

½ CUP DRIED CANNELLINI BEANS, SOAKED OVERNIGHT OR FOR AT LEAST 6 HOURS IN COLD WATER TO COVER

1 SMALL ONION, PEELED

1 FRESH SAGE SPRIG

6 TABLESPOONS EXTRA VIRGIN OLIVE OIL

1 GARLIC CLOVE, PEELED AND SMASHED

½ POUND SMALL CALAMARI, CLEANED, RINSED, AND CUT INTO RINGS

1 CUP DRY WHITE WINE

ONE 14½-OUNCE CAN CRUSHED TOMATOES, DRAINED

1 TABLESPOON CHOPPED FRESH FLAT-LEAF PARSLEY

FRESHLY GROUND BLACK PEPPER

½ POUND MEDIUM SHRIMP, SHELLED AND DEVEINED

1 POUND LITTLENECK CLAMS, SCRUBBED AND RINSED (SEE NOTE)

1 Bring a pot of lightly salted water to a boil. Add the barley, reduce the heat, and simmer until the barley is cooked but still a bit al dente, about 25 minutes. Drain the barley and set aside.

2 Drain and rinse the beans. Bring a pot of lightly salted water to a boil. Add the beans, whole onion, and sage, lower the heat, and simmer until the beans are cooked but still a bit al dente, about 45 minutes. Remove the pot from the heat and let the beans sit in the cooking liquid.

3 Heat 2 tablespoons of the olive oil in a large flameproof casserole over medium-high heat. Add the garlic and calamari and sauté for 2 to 3 minutes. Add half the wine and cook until it evaporates, about 3 minutes. Stir in the tomatoes and parsley and season with salt and pepper. Cook for 5 minutes, then add the shrimp. Cook for 2 more minutes, then remove from the heat and set aside.

4 Pour 2 tablespoons olive oil and wine into a skillet and warm over high heat. Add the clams, cover with a lid, and cook until the clam shells "pop," about 3 minutes.

5 Remove the skillet from the heat and, when the clams are cool enough to handle, discard any clams that have not opened. Remove one-third of the clams and set aside. Remove and discard the shells from the remaining two-thirds of the clams and add

the shelled clams to the casserole with the calamari and shrimp, along with the clams' cooking liquid.

6 Add the barley and beans to the casserole, using a slotted spoon to remove the beans from their cooking liquid. If necessary, add some of the beans' cooking liquid to give the soup an appealing consistency.

7 Return the casserole to the stove and bring to a boil over high heat. Immediately lower the heat and simmer for 5 minutes. Taste and adjust the seasoning if necessary. Just before serving, finish with the remaining 2 tablespoons olive oil and the reserved clams in their shells.

VINO This herbaceous soup calls for a good, woody, not-too-old California Chardonnay.

HOW TO PREPARE AND ENJOY LITTLENECK CLAMS
Sand can become trapped in the shells of littleneck clams. To draw it out, scrub the clams and then soak them in cool salted water for 1 hour. When ready to proceed, drain the saltwater from the bowl and rinse the clams in cold running water.

SPELT AND SEMOLINA GNOCCHI WITH GORGONZOLA SAUCE

SERVES 4 AS AN APPETIZER OR 6 AS A MAIN COURSE

IL CLASSICO

Traditionally, gnocchi is made with potato and semolina flour. My favorite way to serve it is alla Romana, or gratinéed with cheese.

LA MIA VERSIONE

Here farro (spelt) adds a surprising crunchy element to the texture of the gnocchi, and the Gorgonzola stands up to the texture with an assertively flavorful sauce. Gorgonzola loves toasted walnuts, so by all means toss some crumbled into the dish just before serving.

¼ CUP SPELT, SOAKED IN COLD WATER TO COVER FOR 2 HOURS AND DRAINED

FINE SEA SALT

5 CUPS WHOLE MILK

1½ CUPS SEMOLINA FLOUR

3 LARGE EGG YOLKS

¼ CUP FRESHLY GRATED PARMIGIANO-REGGIANO

1 TABLESPOON UNSALTED BUTTER, PLUS MORE FOR GREASING PARCHMENT PAPER AND BAKING DISH

PINCH OF FRESHLY GRATED NUTMEG

FRESHLY GROUND BLACK PEPPER

¾ CUP HALF-AND-HALF

7 OUNCES GORGONZOLA

1 Place the spelt in a pot and cover with cold water. Salt the water, bring it to a boil over high heat, then lower the heat and simmer until the spelt is al dente, about 20 minutes. Drain the spelt and set it aside.

2 Pour the milk into a small pot and bring it to a boil over high heat. Immediately begin pouring the semolina into the milk slowly, whisking continuously until smooth in texture. (If you don't begin adding the flour right away, the milk will boil over.) Add the spelt, continuing to whisk. Lower the heat to very low and cook for about 5 minutes, stirring to prevent scorching.

3 Remove the pot from the heat and fold in the egg yolks, Parmigiano, butter, and nutmeg. Season with salt and pepper.

4 Line a rimmed cookie sheet or baking tray with parchment paper and lightly grease it with butter. Turn the mixture out onto this sheet and use a spatula to spread it out to an even thickness of ¾ inch. Let cool, then cut into 2- or 3-inch rounds using a glass, cutter, or mold.

5 Grease a baking dish with butter and arrange the gnocchi in an overlapping pattern in the dish.

6 Preheat the oven to 375°F.

7 Pour some water into the bottom of a double boiler and bring to a boil over high heat. Pour the half-and-half into the top of the double boiler, add the Gorgonzola, and place over the boiling water. Cook, stirring, until a thick cream is formed. Season with black pepper and pour this cream over the gnocchi.

8 Place the baking dish in the oven and bake until golden brown, about 20 minutes. Remove from the oven, divide among individual plates, and serve.

VINO Whenever I think of Gorgonzola, my mind goes right for a bottle of Piedmontese Barolo, at least five years old, or a less expensive Dolcetto or Nebbiolo.

ROUGHLY CUT PASTA WITH WHITE BEAN SAUCE

——

SERVES 4 AS AN APPETIZER OR 6 AS A MAIN COURSE

IL CLASSICO

Maltagliati is one of the most amusingly descriptive Italian food names. It literally means "grossly cut" and refers to the deliberately inconsistent shape of a pasta that's often made from leftover dough and used in soups, especially pasta e fagioli (pasta and bean soup).

LA MIA VERSIONE

In this twist on pasta e fagioli, the soup becomes a thick sauce for maltagliati, making the pasta the center of the dish rather than vice versa. If you're a seafood lover, toss in some sautéed shrimp and/or scallops during the last few seconds of cooking.

MALTAGLIATI DOUGH

SEMOLINA FLOUR FOR DUSTING THE WORK SURFACE

½ POUND (ABOUT 2 CUPS) DURUM FLOUR (SEE IN SEARCH OF . . . , PAGE 16) OR ALL-PURPOSE FLOUR

½ POUND (ABOUT 2 CUPS) ALL-PURPOSE FLOUR

FINE SEA SALT

1 Dust a clean work surface with semolina flour. Sift the flours and salt together on this surface. Gather them into a mound and make a well in the center. Slowly pour ½ cup hot tap water into the center and mix it in a circle with your fingers or a fork, working your way out toward the edges and adding more water a little at a time as it is absorbed. Knead the dough until it is firm and elastic. (You can also make the dough in a standing mixer, using the hook attachment.)

2 Run the dough through a pasta machine as many times as necessary to obtain a sheet less than ⅛ inch thick. (If you don't own a pasta machine, use a rolling pin, but take care to roll the pasta evenly.) Gingerly stack the pasta sheets, roll them up, and cut at an angle to form diamond shapes measuring about 1½ x 1½ inches. This is your maltagliati.

3 Line a cookie sheet with wax paper and dust it with semolina flour. Spread the maltagliati out on the sheet. Set aside.

CANNELLINI BEAN RAGÙ AND ASSEMBLY

1 Drain and rinse the beans, transfer them to a pot, add the whole onion, unpeeled garlic clove, 4 of the sage leaves, and a pinch of salt. Fill the pot with plenty of water, bring to a boil over high heat, then lower the heat and simmer until the beans are cooked but still a bit al dente, 40 to 45 minutes. Remove the pot from the heat and allow the beans to cool in the cooking liquid. (If the beans seem soft after soaking, cook them in a wider pot; they will cook more quickly if spread out.)

2 Bring a large pot of salted water to a boil over high heat.

3 Warm ¼ cup of the olive oil and the sliced garlic in a sauté pan over medium-high heat. Add the red pepper and remaining sage leaves. When the garlic turns golden, 4 to 5 minutes, add the diced tomatoes, season with salt and black pepper, and stir in the beans using a slotted spoon to remove them from their cooking liquid. Add a small ladleful of the bean's cooking liquid.

4 Add the pasta to the boiling water. Cook for 2 to 3 minutes, then use a slotted spoon to transfer the pasta from the pot to the sauté pan with the ragù. Stir well and add the rest of the olive oil and a few tablespoons of the cooking water from the pasta. (The sauce should be soupy.) Taste and add salt, if necessary, then finish with a few grinds of black pepper. Divide among individual plates or bowls and serve.

VINO This dish makes me think of the early fall and a good, young, light Burgundy.

HOW TO STORE FRESH PASTA

To store fresh pasta, dust it with cornmeal, stack or gather it in bunches, and carefully fold it over on itself until you get it down to a manageable size. Wrap snugly in plastic wrap and refrigerate until ready to use.

½ CUP DRIED CANNELLINI BEANS, SOAKED OVERNIGHT OR FOR AT LEAST 6 HOURS IN COLD WATER TO COVER

1 SMALL ONION, PEELED

5 GARLIC CLOVES, 1 UNPEELED, 4 PEELED AND THINLY SLICED

10 FRESH SAGE LEAVES

FINE SEA SALT

½ CUP EXTRA VIRGIN OLIVE OIL

PINCH OF HOT RED PEPPER FLAKES

4 PLUM TOMATOES, PEELED (SEE NOTE ON PAGE 25) AND DICED

FRESHLY GROUND BLACK PEPPER

SPELT WITH CALAMARI, TOMATO, AND SPICY GREENS

SERVES 6 AS AN APPETIZER

IL CLASSICO

Zimino is a Livornese dish, usually reserved for squid or cuttlefish (seppie in zimino), that uses oil, spinach, tomato, and lots of minced garlic to create a spicy stew. It's particularly effective for flavoring relatively neutral-flavored seafood that can soak up the garlic's intense flavor.

LA MIA VERSIONE

This recipe stirs a conventional seppie in zimino into a farrotto, creating a sort of spicy Italian answer to paella as the grain takes on the color of the tomatoes and the peppery flavor of the dandelion greens. Note that you need to soak the spelt for two hours before you begin making this dish.

ZIMINO

¼ CUP EXTRA VIRGIN OLIVE OIL

⅓ CUP CHOPPED ONION

¼ CUP MINCED CARROT

¼ CUP CHOPPED CELERY

2 GARLIC CLOVES, CHOPPED

1 POUND FRESH CALAMARI, CLEANED, RINSED, BODIES SLICED ¼ INCH WIDE

FINE SEA SALT

¼ TEASPOON HOT RED PEPPER FLAKES

1 CUP RED WINE

1 CUP DICED CANNED IMPORTED ITALIAN TOMATOES, FROM ABOUT 2 CANNED TOMATOES

1 POUND FRESH DANDELION GREENS OR ARUGULA, CLEANED, RINSED, SPUN DRY, AND SLICED INTO 1-INCH-WIDE STRIPS

1 Pour half the olive oil into a medium flameproof casserole and warm over medium-high heat. Add the onion, carrot, and celery and sauté until translucent, about 5 minutes. Add the garlic, stir, and sauté until browned, about another 3 minutes.

2 Stir in the calamari and season with salt and red pepper. Sauté for 5 minutes. Add the wine and cook until evaporated, about 3 minutes.

3 Add the tomatoes, stir, and cook for 5 more minutes. Top the mixture with the dandelion greens, cover with a lid, reduce the heat to very low, and simmer for 30 minutes. Remove the lid, stir, taste, and adjust the seasoning if necessary. Stir in the remaining olive oil and cook for another 10 minutes. Cover to keep warm and set aside.

(continued)

¼ CUP EXTRA VIRGIN OLIVE OIL

3 CUPS SPELT, SOAKED IN COLD WATER TO COVER FOR 2 HOURS AND DRAINED

½ CUP RED WINE

10 CUPS VEGETABLE STOCK, SIMMERING IN A POT ON A BACK BURNER

FINE SEA SALT

1 Heat 3 tablespoons of the olive oil in a wide heavy saucepan over medium-high heat. When the olive oil is almost smoking, add the spelt and stir until it has absorbed all the oil. Pour in the wine and cook until it evaporates, about 2 minutes.

2 Add a few ladlefuls of the stock. Cook the spelt, stirring often to prevent sticking and adding a ladle of stock every time the liquid is absorbed.

3 After 10 minutes, add the calamari mixture, stirring well but gently, and continue adding stock as necessary. The spelt will be done after 25 to 30 minutes. Add the remaining olive oil and stir energetically to make the farrotto very creamy. Season with salt, and serve at once.

VINO A robust Merlot from Oregon is the perfect foil for this dish's spiciness.

SOFT POLENTA WITH PORK SAUSAGE AND TRUFFLE SAUCE

SERVES 6 AS A MAIN COURSE

IL CLASSICO

In classic Tuscan cuisine, polenta often takes the place of pasta, offering a different but no less satisfying way of rounding out a dish and soaking up a sauce.

LA MIA VERSIONE

In this recipe we use polenta to replace the fresh pasta that would normally accompany norcina, an ancient pork and cranberry bean ragù from the border between Umbria and Tuscany, where black truffles are found. This is my version of norcina, which omits the beans.

1 Pour the olive oil into a flameproof casserole and warm over medium-high heat. Add the onion, celery, and carrot, season with salt and pepper, and sauté very slowly until caramelized, about 8 minutes.

2 Meanwhile, crumble the sausage by hand and add it to another sauté pan. Cook over low heat until the meat is browned and the fat is rendered. Drain off the fat and add the sausage to the pan with the vegetables. Use a whisk or fork to break up the sausage even more.

3 Add the Marsala, raise the heat to medium-high, and let it evaporate, about 2 minutes.

4 Drain the porcini in a fine-mesh strainer set over a bowl. Strain the soaking liquid through a double layer of cheesecloth set over another bowl. Set the strained liquid aside.

5 Roughly chop the porcini and add them to the casserole. Stir well and cook for 10 minutes. Add the truffle and the porcini-soaking liquid and cook very slowly for an hour. If the sauce becomes dry, add a little chicken stock.

(continued)

3 TABLESPOONS EXTRA VIRGIN OLIVE OIL

1 MEDIUM ONION, CHOPPED

1 CELERY RIB, CHOPPED

1 CARROT, CHOPPED

FINE SEA SALT

FRESHLY GROUND BLACK PEPPER

2 POUNDS SWEET SAUSAGE, CASINGS REMOVED

¾ CUP DRY MARSALA

¾ CUP DRIED PORCINI, SOAKED IN 2 CUPS WARM WATER FOR 1 HOUR

1 BLACK TRUFFLE (ABOUT 1 OUNCE), VERY FINELY DICED, CANNED IF FRESH ARE NOT AVAILABLE

1 CUP CHICKEN STOCK

FINE SEA SALT TO TASTE

1¼ CUPS QUICK-COOKING POLENTA

1 CUP WATER, SIMMERING IN A POT ON A BACK BURNER

1 TABLESPOON EXTRA VIRGIN OLIVE OIL

1 You can either use the instructions on the package or follow this procedure: pour 6 cups water into a deep heavy pan and salt it lightly. Bring to a boil over high heat. Reduce the heat to medium and, beating continually with a whisk, add the polenta slowly and gradually. Stir constantly as you cook the polenta, until it reaches the consistency of a creamy porridge, about 5 minutes. Add some of the simmering water if the polenta becomes too thick. Stir in salt to taste and the olive oil, then cover and set the polenta aside in a warm place until you are ready to serve.

2 Serve the polenta from a big serving plate topped with the norcina sauce or from individual plates.

IN SEARCH OF . . . DRIED PORCINI MUSHROOMS

Dried porcini are one of the mainstays of any Italian kitchen. They offer a way to add intense porcino flavor to soups and sauces all year long. While they don't match the textural voluptuousness of fresh porcini, they compensate with a versatile by-product: the soaking liquid produced when they are reconstituted can add great flavor to recipes. Keep this trick in mind when making a mushroom risotto; use the soaking liquid in place of the last addition of stock. (The less water you use, the more flavorful the soaking liquid will be.)

VINO Select a young Rosso di Montalcino, the Brunello table wine made with grapes from the year's first harvest (the younger the better), from Tuscany.

FUNGHI
MUSHROOMS

When autumn arrives in Tuscany, its forests of pines, chestnut trees, and giant oaks are blanketed by a low-lying fog known as *la brina*. The mysterious aura of la brina is increased by the magical overnight appearance of *funghi*, or mushrooms, which grow in these forests, in the shadow of those trees, conjured into being by the moisture itself.

Because really flavorful mushrooms have never been domesticated, you don't farm them; you *forage* for them. They have to be searched for, and it's an enduring tribute to our collective love for them that generation after generation of people have found them to be worth the effort. In classic Tuscan cuisine mushrooms play a role similar to the one they play in nature—they disappear into their surroundings, vanishing into sauces and soups or being casually tossed into a stew.

This is how I came to know mushrooms. As a child there was only one mushroom in my life, the porcino, king of mushrooms, and the only one that my mother ever cooked. She sautéed porcini with olive oil, garlic, and rosemary and served them as a *contorno* (vegetable side dish), or diced them up as an element in any number of sauces.

When I ventured away from home and began to travel throughout Italy, I discovered other mushrooms. Black trumpets, pleurotes, and chanterelles. I also got to know the rarest of mushrooms, ovoli, which were made into a memorable salad.

I have come to love experimenting with mushrooms. I love hen of the woods with cold cuts. I love chanterelles with clams. I love pastas and salads built around mushrooms. And I love reconstituting dried mushrooms in various liquids, like red wine or any number of stocks.

When I first became a restaurateur in the United States, I was so eager to share my love of mushrooms that I discovered a new form of foraging by telephone as I called all over the world looking for the ones I remembered. They're easier to obtain now, but I've always felt lucky to have access to them and their transporting powers—every bite seems to return me to the dark woods of Tuscany in the early morning, or is it early evening? I can't tell. I only know that I'm happy to be here.

FUNGHI FRITTI
FRIED MUSHROOMS

———

SERVES 6 AS AN APPETIZER OR 4 AS A SIDE DISH

IL CLASSICO

In the traditional Tuscan kitchen, mushrooms being prepared for frying are dredged either in flour or in a batter of egg yolks and bread crumbs.

LA MIA VERSIONE

This recipe is lighter than the original thanks to a batter of rice flour, wine, water, and beer. It also encourages you to combine a variety of mushrooms, which Tuscans traditionally tend not to do. Serve this with Florentine steak (see headnotes on pages 51 and 208).

2 POUNDS MIXED MUSHROOMS, SUCH AS OYSTER, SHIITAKE, CREMINI, WIPED CLEAN, STEMS TRIMMED

¾ POUND (ABOUT 3 CUPS) RICE FLOUR

1½ CUPS DRY WHITE WINE

1 CUP SPARKLING WATER

⅓ CUP LIGHT BEER

1 TABLESPOON FINELY CHOPPED FRESH HERBS, SUCH AS ROSEMARY, THYME, SAGE

FINE SEA SALT

FRESHLY GROUND BLACK PEPPER

VEGETABLE OIL FOR FRYING

1 Slice the larger mushrooms into 1-inch pieces, leaving the smaller ones whole.

2 In a large bowl, whisk together the rice flour, wine, sparkling water, and beer until a light batter is formed. Stir in the herbs and season with salt and pepper.

3 Pour oil into a large deep sauté pan to a depth of 1 inch and heat it over medium-high heat to 375°F. (A drop of water flicked into the oil will sizzle on contact.) Dip the mushrooms in the batter, then fry them in the oil in batches until crispy, about 3 minutes. Remove them from the oil with tongs or a slotted spoon and drain on paper towels. Sprinkle with salt and serve right away.

VINO These mushrooms—crunchy outside and soft inside—call for a Super Tuscan. Here's a tip: don't pick one with a black rooster on the label, which indicates a Chianti . . . not what you want here. A good reserve Cabernet Sauvignon from California would also be delicious.

PICKLED MUSHROOM AND CHICKPEA SALAD

SERVES 6 AS AN APPETIZER OR 8 AS A SIDE DISH

IL CLASSICO

Chickpeas, one of the most popular Mediterranean ingredients, and pickled mushrooms are two mainstays of the Tuscan antipasto table, where the chickpea's starch and the mushroom's acidic pickling liquid offer relief from the salty meats and cheeses.

LA MIA VERSIONE

Although they often appear side by side, mushrooms and chickpeas are not traditionally tossed together in a salad. It turns out that they perfectly complement one another, even when meats and cheeses are nowhere to be found. This recipe is also useful for the pickled mushrooms alone, which can be served as an hors d'oeuvre and are a perfect match with an ice-cold martini. This is a great side dish for game or duck.

Note that you need to make the pickled mushrooms a day or two before you serve this salad.

3 CUPS DRY WHITE WINE

1 CUP WHITE WINE VINEGAR

2 GARLIC CLOVES, PEELED

2 BAY LEAVES

1 TEASPOON WHOLE BLACK PEPPERCORNS

FINE SEA SALT

3 CUPS WHITE BUTTON MUSHROOMS, STEMS TRIMMED AND WIPED CLEAN

1 CUP EXTRA VIRGIN OLIVE OIL

MUSHROOMS

1 Pour the wine and vinegar into a flameproof casserole. Add the garlic, bay leaves, and peppercorns. Season with salt and bring to a boil over high heat. Lower the heat and simmer for about 10 minutes. Lower the mushrooms into the liquid, raise the heat, return the liquid to a boil, and cook for 2 minutes. Remove the mushrooms from the liquid using a slotted spoon and let them dry on a clean towel.

2 Drain the cooking liquid and reserve the solids.

3 When dry, transfer the mushrooms to a glass jar. Add the reserved bay leaves, peppercorns, and garlic. Fill the jar with olive oil until the mushrooms are completely covered, then seal the jar and store it in the refrigerator. The mushrooms will be ready to serve after they have been infused for 24 hours but will gain more flavor over a few days.

(continued)

1½ CUPS DRIED CHICKPEAS, SOAKED
OVERNIGHT OR FOR AT LEAST 6 HOURS IN
COLD WATER TO COVER

FINE SEA SALT

1 FRESH ROSEMARY SPRIG

2 GARLIC CLOVES

¾ CUP HALVED CHERRY TOMATOES

FRESHLY GROUND BLACK PEPPER

CHICKPEAS

Drain the chickpeas. Transfer them to a pot and cover by twice their volume with cold water. Generously salt the water and add the rosemary and garlic. Bring to a boil over high heat, then lower the heat and simmer for about 1 hour, until cooked through but still firm. Remove from the heat and allow the chickpeas to cool in the cooking liquid, then drain them. Pick out and discard the garlic and rosemary sprig.

ASSEMBLY

Transfer the drained chickpeas to a bowl. Remove the mushrooms from the oil and add them to the bowl along with the cherry tomatoes. Toss with 2 teaspoons of the oil from the jar, season with salt and pepper, and toss thoroughly but gently.

VINO This light dish calls for the smoothest of all Piemontese wines, a Dolcetto. Either a young or an aged one will work well here.

TAGLIATA DI PORCINI ALLA FIORENTINA

SLICED PORCINI MUSHROOMS, FLORENTINE STYLE

SERVES 4 AS A FIRST COURSE OR SIDE DISH

IL CLASSICO

When one speaks of bistecca alla Fiorentina, one speaks of a supreme porterhouse steak, at least two inches thick, cooked over an open flame, sliced, and drizzled with an excellent-quality olive oil.

LA MIA VERSIONE

This recipe gives mushrooms the bistecca treatment by slicing large porcini or portobellos and drizzling them with a hot garlic sauce. This is delicious on its own or as a side dish with steak.

1 Preheat the oven to 300°F.

2 Wrap the garlic in aluminum foil and bake until soft, about 1 hour. (Test for doneness by inserting a sharp, thin-bladed knife into a clove. It should pass right through to the center.) Remove the garlic from the oven and let cool.

3 Squeeze the pulp out of the garlic skins and place it in a blender. Add the mustard, thyme, and 5 tablespoons of the olive oil. Process for about 30 seconds, until smooth and homogenous.

4 Remove the stems from the porcini, peel them with a peeler, and slice them lengthwise about ½ inch wide. Clean the caps with a damp towel. Lightly brush the caps and stems with the remaining 2 tablespoons olive oil.

5 Warm a nonstick pan over medium heat. Add the mushroom caps and stems and cook for 3 to 4 minutes per side. Season to taste with salt and pepper, then remove from the pan.

6 Slice the mushroom caps lengthwise into pieces about ½ inch wide. Arrange the slices and stems on a hot plate and drizzle with the garlic sauce.

VINO A full-bodied fruity Merlot, preferably from Australia, is the perfect complement to this dish.

2 WHOLE HEADS GARLIC

2 TEASPOONS DIJON MUSTARD

LEAVES FROM 1 SMALL BUNCH FRESH THYME

¼ CUP PLUS 3 TABLESPOONS EXTRA VIRGIN OLIVE OIL

8 LARGE PORCINI MUSHROOMS OR PORTOBELLO CAPS

FINE SEA SALT

FRESHLY GROUND BLACK PEPPER

TUSCAN-STYLE PORCINI MUSHROOMS

SERVES 4 AS AN APPETIZER

IL CLASSICO

In poorer Italian families, mothers looking to treat their children to a meal beyond their means ask the butcher for a cut of meat called *fettina,* a negligibly thin strip that most would discard but that Tuscan mamas are expert at elevating with intense, intuitive seasoning and a quick pan-searing.

LA MIA VERSIONE

Here we apply the fettina principle to meaty porcini mushroom caps, which drink up the flavor of the marinade just like the fettina does.

4 LARGE, FIRM FRESH PORCINI MUSHROOMS

¼ CUP EXTRA VIRGIN OLIVE OIL

4 GARLIC CLOVES, SLICED

8 FRESH BASIL LEAVES

FINE SEA SALT

FRESHLY GROUND BLACK PEPPER

1 Remove the mushroom stems, peel them with a peeler, and slice them on the bias about ¼ inch thick. Clean the caps with a damp towel.

2 Pour 2 tablespoons of the olive oil into a large skillet and heat it over medium-high heat. Add the garlic and sauté until golden, about 1 minute. Add the mushroom stems and basil leaves, then the caps. Season with salt and pepper and turn the mushrooms over. Cook for 2 to 3 minutes, drizzle with the remaining 2 tablespoons of the olive oil, and serve.

VINO Splurge for a Nebbiolo, the classic Piemonte wine, to go with the big flavors and elevate the experience even more. The younger the wine, the better.

SPICY MUSHROOM SOUP WITH EGG, BREAD, AND CHEESE

———

SERVES 4 AS AN APPETIZER OR A SOUP

IL CLASSICO

Zuppa alla Pavese is a simple main dish from Lombardy made by pouring hot broth over eggs, bread, and cheese.

LA MIA VERSIONE

A soulfully seasoned, slightly spicy stew of mushrooms, red pepper flakes, and thyme dramatically alters the character of this soup. The egg is the defining ingredient of the original recipe, but here it merely adds richness to an already satisfying mixture.

---

2 TABLESPOONS EXTRA VIRGIN OLIVE OIL

2 GARLIC CLOVES, THINLY SLICED

PINCH OF HOT RED PEPPER FLAKES

3 CUPS TIGHTLY PACKED MIXED FRESH MUSHROOMS, STEMS REMOVED, WIPED CLEAN WITH A DAMP CLOTH

LEAVES OF 4 FRESH THYME SPRIGS

FINE SEA SALT

FRESHLY GROUND BLACK PEPPER

½ CUP CANNED CRUSHED TOMATOES WITH THEIR LIQUID

1 QUART VEGETABLE STOCK, SIMMERING IN A POT ON A BACK BURNER

FOUR 1-INCH-THICK SLICES TUSCAN COUNTRY BREAD, GRILLED OR TOASTED

4 LARGE EGGS

¼ CUP GRATED PARMIGIANO-REGGIANO

1 Heat the olive oil in a wide flameproof casserole over medium-high heat. Add the garlic and sauté until browned, about 3 minutes. Add the red pepper and the mushrooms, then the thyme leaves. Stir well and season with salt and pepper. Cook for 5 minutes.

2 Add the tomatoes, taste and adjust the seasoning, and cook for an additional 5 minutes.

3 Add the stock, raise the heat to high, bring to a boil, then lower the heat and simmer for 20 minutes.

4 Place a slice of bread in each of 4 bowls. Break the eggs carefully into the bowls on top of the bread, then top each egg with 1 tablespoon Parmigiano. Carefully ladle the hot soup over the egg and crouton and serve.

VINO A full-bodied Dolcetto will have a great affinity for the mushrooms.

ZUPPA DI FUNGHI

CREAMLESS MUSHROOM SOUP

———

SERVES 4 TO 6 AS AN APPETIZER

IL CLASSICO

Cacciucco di funghi is a dish made by Tuscans who live too far from the coast to obtain fresh seafood. They apply the principles of a cacciucco (page 7) to a hearty soup that replaces shellfish with mushrooms, something they have in great abundance.

LA MIA VERSIONE

This recipe adds potato to the recipe for cacciucco di funghi to create a thick and creamy mushroom soup without any cream.

---

2 POUNDS PLUM TOMATOES, HALVED LENGTHWISE

2 TABLESPOONS FINE SEA SALT

2 TEASPOONS SUGAR

3 FRESH ROSEMARY SPRIGS

6 FRESH THYME SPRIGS

6 GARLIC CLOVES, SLICED

12 FRESH BASIL LEAVES, TORN BY HAND

OVEN-DRIED TOMATO PUREE

1 Preheat the oven to 300°F and keep the door slightly ajar with a cork or other flame-proof item to help circulate the air.

2 Line a rimmed cookie sheet with parchment paper and arrange the tomato halves on it in a single layer. Mix the salt and sugar together in a small bowl and sprinkle the tomatoes with the mixture. Then sprinkle with the rosemary, thyme, garlic, and basil.

3 Place the rimmed cookie sheet in the oven and bake for 90 minutes, until the tomatoes are dried but not shriveled.

4 Remove the cookie sheet from the oven. Use tongs to pick off and discard the garlic and herbs. While the tomatoes are still warm, puree them in a food processor. Set aside while you make the soup.

1 Pour enough olive oil (approximately 2 tablespoons) into a flameproof casserole to generously coat the bottom. Warm over medium-high heat. Add the onion, minced garlic, and red pepper and cook until the onion is browned, about 4 minutes.

2 Add the potato, season with salt, cook for 2 to 3 minutes, then stir in the tomato puree. Cook for 5 more minutes, then add the simmering stock. Taste and adjust the seasoning if necessary. Cook until the potatoes are cooked through, about 5 more minutes.

3 Blend the soup with an immersion blender or ladle it into a blender or food processor and process until creamy. (Be sure to leave the top piece of the blender out to allow steam to escape and be very careful when blending this, or any, hot liquid.) Return to the casserole and set aside.

4 Pour enough olive oil (approximately 2 tablespoons) into a wide deep skillet to coat the bottom. Warm the oil over medium-high heat. Add the sliced garlic and rosemary and sauté until the garlic is browned, about 1 minute. Stir in the mushrooms, season with salt and black pepper, and sauté until the mushrooms are wilted, about 3 minutes. Use tongs to fish out and discard the rosemary, then add the mushrooms to the soup.

5 Place the casserole over low heat and let the soup simmer for 15 to 20 minutes. Taste, adjust the seasoning if necessary, and finish with a drizzle of extra virgin olive oil. Ladle into bowls and serve hot.

VINO This recipe, inspired by the cuisine of the southern tip of Tuscany, suggests a fairly dry red wine, so go with a Morellino.

EXTRA VIRGIN OLIVE OIL

1 SMALL ONION, CHOPPED

2 GARLIC CLOVES, MINCED

PINCH OF HOT RED PEPPER FLAKES

1 LARGE IDAHO POTATO, PEELED AND CUT INTO 1-INCH CUBES

FINE SEA SALT

5 CUPS VEGETABLE STOCK, SIMMERING IN A POT ON A BACK BURNER

2 GARLIC CLOVES, SLICED

1 FRESH ROSEMARY SPRIG

1½ POUNDS MIXED WILD MUSHROOMS, SUCH AS CHANTERELLE, BLACK TRUMPET, AND PLEUROTE, STEMS REMOVED, LARGE ONES QUARTERED, SMALL ONES HALVED OR LEFT WHOLE

FRESHLY GROUND BLACK PEPPER

TOMATO AND MUSHROOM BREAD SOUP

———

SERVES 6 AS AN APPETIZER OR 8 AS A SIDE DISH

IL CLASSICO

Mushrooms and tomatoes are often featured together in braising liquids, as in a stracotto Fiorentino (page 222), which is essentially an Italian pot roast.

LA MIA VERSIONE

This recipe makes the hearty flavor of the braising liquid in stracotto the focus of the dish and turns an old-fashioned meat dish into a new-style bread soup.

1¼ CUPS EXTRA VIRGIN OLIVE OIL

1 ONION, CHOPPED

½ CARROT, CHOPPED

½ CELERY RIB, CHOPPED

2 GARLIC CLOVES, MINCED

2½ POUNDS VINE-RIPENED TOMATOES, COARSELY CHOPPED

24 FRESH BASIL LEAVES, TORN BY HAND

1 POUND STALE BREAD

6 CUPS VEGETABLE STOCK

FINE SEA SALT

FRESHLY GROUND BLACK PEPPER

1 POUND MIXED FRESH MUSHROOMS, STEMS REMOVED, COARSELY CHOPPED

LEAVES FROM 3 FRESH THYME SPRIGS

1 Pour ½ cup of the olive oil into a casserole and warm it over medium heat. Add the onion, carrot, celery, and 1 clove of minced garlic and cook until the onion is translucent, 3 to 4 minutes.

2 Add the tomatoes and cook for about 30 minutes, lowering the heat to let the liquid simmer.

3 Remove from the heat and add half of the basil. Puree in a food processor. (Be sure to leave the top piece of the processor out to allow steam to escape and be very careful when blending this, or any, hot liquid.)

4 Cut off and discard the bread crusts. Cut the bread into ½-inch cubes. If the bread is not completely stale, dry the cubes on a cookie sheet in a preheated 300°F oven until it is completely dry, but do not let it color or burn.

5 Pour the vegetable stock into a large flameproof casserole and bring to a boil over high heat. Stir in the tomato sauce. When the liquid returns to a boil, lower the heat and add the bread, remaining basil, and ¼ cup of the remaining olive oil. Season with salt and pepper and simmer, stirring frequently.

6 Meanwhile, pour ¼ cup of the remaining olive oil into a skillet and warm it over medium-high heat. Add the remaining clove of minced garlic to the skillet and brown it, about 1 minute. Add the mushrooms and thyme and sauté for 5 minutes, seasoning with salt and pepper, then stir the mushrooms into the soup.

7 Simmer the soup, stirring frequently, until the bread has fallen apart and thickened it, about 15 minutes. Remove from the heat, add the remaining ¼ cup olive oil, taste, adjust the seasoning if necessary, and serve at once.

VINO A young, slightly fruity Sauvignon, preferably from the Veneto, will complement these flavors.

HOT SALAD OF MUSHROOMS, SPELT, AND ARUGULA

———

SERVES 4 AS AN APPETIZER

IL CLASSICO

Farro (or spelt, a grain you can read about on page 23) is traditionally used in soups, in farrotto, or in a panzanella di farro, a bread salad with al dente farro in place of stale bread.

LA MIA VERSIONE

This recipe—a true original that we've served in my restaurants for years—makes spelt the basis of a warm salad in which mushrooms and bacon are sautéed and added hot to a bowl with arugula and spelt. The greens wilt ever so slightly, and the flavors melt together effortlessly.

6 TABLESPOONS EXTRA VIRGIN OLIVE OIL

½ MEDIUM ONION, THINLY SLICED

2 CUPS SPELT, SOAKED IN COLD WATER TO COVER FOR 2 HOURS AND DRAINED

2 GARLIC CLOVES, PEELED AND PRESSED FLAT

½ POUND OYSTER MUSHROOMS, CLEANED WITH A DAMP CLOTH AND SLICED INTO THIN STRIPS

½ POUND CREMINI MUSHROOMS, CLEANED WITH A DAMP CLOTH AND SLICED INTO THIN STRIPS

FINE SEA SALT

FRESHLY GROUND BLACK PEPPER

2 OUNCES SLAB BACON, CUT INTO THIN STRIPS OR SMALL CUBES

1 BUNCH ARUGULA, STEMS TRIMMED, WASHED, AND DRIED

1 Warm 2 tablespoons of the olive oil in a sauté pan over medium-high heat. Add the onion and sauté until golden, about 4 minutes. Add the spelt, stir, and add enough water to cover by 1 inch. Lower the heat and cook, covered, for 20 minutes or until the spelt has absorbed the water. Set aside.

2 Warm another 2 tablespoons olive oil in a sauté pan over medium-high heat. Add the garlic and cook until golden, about 4 minutes. Remove and discard the garlic. Add the oyster mushrooms, cremini mushrooms, 1 teaspoon sea salt, and 1 teaspoon black pepper. Stir and sauté until the mushrooms are softened, about 5 minutes. Set aside.

3 Place the bacon in a sauté pan and cook over low heat until the fat is rendered and the bacon is browned. Pour off the fat.

4 Transfer the bacon to a large salad bowl. Add the spelt and mushrooms and toss well. Add the arugula leaves, the remaining 2 tablespoons olive oil, 1 teaspoon sea salt, and 1 teaspoon black pepper. Toss well and serve at once.

VINO Wash down this peppery salad with Traminer, a crisp white wine from Friuli or Trentino.

MUSHROOM TIMBALE

——

SERVES 6 AS AN APPETIZER OR 4 AS A MAIN COURSE

IL CLASSICO

A timpano is a molded dish made with pasta and other ingredients that is inverted and unmolded just before serving. The dish was immortalized for Americans in the film *Big Night,* in which it practically starred. It's a real showstopper.

LA MIA VERSIONE

This recipe uses a bundt mold to add an extra dimension to the mushroom timpano: a mushroom and tomato sauce is spooned into the center of the unmolded dish.

MUSHROOM SAUCE

1 Soak the porcini in 1 cup warm water for 30 minutes. Strain them in a fine-mesh strainer set over a bowl, gently squeezing the porcini by hand to extract as much flavorful liquid as possible. Pass the water through a cheesecloth into a clean bowl, reserving it.

2 Warm 3 tablespoons of the olive oil in a sauté pan over medium heat. Add the shallot and sauté until browned, about 2 minutes. Add the drained porcini and 1 sprig of the rosemary, season with salt and pepper, stir, and cook for 4 to 5 minutes. Add ½ cup of the mushroom-soaking water and the stock; simmer for 15 minutes, then remove from the heat and cool. Remove the mushrooms from the liquid with a slotted spoon and transfer them to a cutting board. Chop them roughly and return them to the liquid.

3 Pour enough olive oil into a wide deep skillet just to cover the bottom. Warm the oil over medium-high heat. Add the garlic and remaining rosemary and sauté until the garlic is browned, about 1 minute. Add the fresh mushrooms and sauté until wilted, about 3 minutes. Season with salt and pepper. (You may need to do this in batches or use 2 pans.) Remove the skillet from the heat and stir in the porcini sauce.

(continued)

2 OUNCES DRIED PORCINI MUSHROOMS

APPROXIMATELY ⅓ CUP EXTRA VIRGIN OLIVE OIL

1 TABLESPOON CHOPPED SHALLOT

4 FRESH ROSEMARY SPRIGS

FINE SEA SALT

FRESHLY GROUND BLACK PEPPER

½ CUP VEGETABLE STOCK

4 GARLIC CLOVES, SLICED

1½ POUNDS MIXED FRESH MUSHROOMS, SUCH AS SHIITAKE, CHANTERELLE, AND OYSTER, LARGER ONES CLEANED AND QUARTERED, SMALL ONES LEFT WHOLE OR HALVED

1 POUND CHERRY TOMATOES, HALVED

3 TEASPOONS FINE SEA SALT

1 TEASPOON SUGAR

1 FRESH ROSEMARY SPRIG

3 FRESH THYME SPRIGS

3 GARLIC CLOVES, SLICED

6 FRESH BASIL LEAVES, TORN BY HAND

1 Preheat the oven to 300°F and keep the door slightly ajar with a cork or other flame-proof item to help circulate the air.

2 Line a rimmed cookie sheet with parchment paper and arrange the tomato halves on it in a single layer. Mix the salt and sugar together in a small bowl and sprinkle the tomatoes with the mixture. Then sprinkle with the rosemary, thyme, garlic, and basil.

3 Place the rimmed cookie sheet in the oven and bake for 90 minutes, until the tomatoes are dried but not shriveled.

4 Remove the pan from the oven and add the tomatoes to the mushroom sauce.

FINE SEA SALT

3 LARGE EGGS, SEPARATED

10 TABLESPOONS UNSALTED BUTTER, 8 TABLESPOONS (1 STICK) MELTED

1 CUP GRATED PARMIGIANO-REGGIANO

1 CUP WHOLE MILK

FRESHLY GROUND BLACK PEPPER

1 POUND FRESH EGG TAGLIARINI

¼ CUP DRIED BREAD CRUMBS

PASTA AND ASSEMBLY

1 Preheat the oven to 325°F.

2 Bring a large pot of salted water to a boil over high heat.

3 Place the egg yolks in a large bowl. Add the melted butter, Parmigiano, and milk, and season with salt and pepper. Whisk until a homogenous mixture is formed.

4 In a separate bowl, whip the egg whites until stiff peaks form.

5 Add the pasta to the boiling salted water and cook it halfway, about 2 minutes. Drain it in a colander, rinse quickly under cold running water to stop the cooking, and transfer the pasta to the bowl with the yolk-cheese-milk mixture. Carefully fold the egg whites into this mixture.

6 Grease a 2-quart bundt mold with 1 tablespoon of the remaining butter and coat it with bread crumbs. Stir half the pasta mixture into the mold, pressing down gently to eliminate any air pockets. Spoon three-quarters of the mushroom-tomato sauce over the pasta. Cover this with the remaining pasta, again pressing down to force out any air. Sprinkle with the remaining bread crumbs and dot with the remaining butter.

7 Place the mold in the preheated oven and bake until golden on top, about 30 minutes.

(continued)

8 Remove from the oven and let rest for 5 minutes. Meanwhile, reheat the remaining mushroom-tomato sauce.

9 Unmold the timpano by covering it with a large plate and inverting the mold and plate simultaneously. Carefully remove the mold.

10 Spoon the mushroom-tomato sauce into the hole in the center of the unmolded timpano and serve from the middle of the table.

VINO Try this with a Dolcetto, which I think of as a "baby" Barolo.

TAGLIARINI WITH SMALL VEAL MEATBALLS, MUSHROOMS, AND SWEET PEAS

——

SERVES 6 AS AN APPETIZER OR 4 AS A PASTA

IL CLASSICO

There's perhaps no more stereotypical Italian-American dish than spaghetti and meatballs. Unfortunately, most Americans associate it with overcooked pasta and oversized, tasteless meatballs drowning in "red sauce."

LA MIA VERSIONE

This dish makes the idea of pasta and meatballs fresh again, with small veal meatballs, fresh tagliarini rather than dried spaghetti, and the addition of mushrooms, sweet peas, and mint—and no tomato sauce. It proves how much flavor and texture mushrooms add to almost any recipe.

¾ POUND GROUND VEAL

¾ CUP GRATED PARMIGIANO-REGGIANO

1 LARGE EGG YOLK

¼ CUP DRIED BREAD CRUMBS

½ GARLIC CLOVE, MINCED

2 TEASPOONS CHOPPED FRESH FLAT-LEAF PARSLEY

FINE SEA SALT

FRESHLY GROUND BLACK PEPPER

CANOLA OIL TO FRY THE MEATBALLS

⅓ CUP EXTRA VIRGIN OLIVE OIL

1 MEDIUM ONION, CHOPPED

4 CUPS WHITE BUTTON MUSHROOMS, STEMS REMOVED, SLICED ¼ INCH THICK

1½ CUPS FRESH SWEET PEAS OR THE SMALLEST POSSIBLE FROZEN PEAS

½ CUP VEGETABLE STOCK

6 FRESH MINT LEAVES

1½ POUNDS FRESH TAGLIARINI

4 TABLESPOONS (½ STICK) UNSALTED BUTTER

(continued)

1 Place the meat in a bowl. Add half of the Parmigiano, the egg yolk, bread crumbs, garlic, and parsley. Season well with salt and pepper and mix thoroughly but delicately so as not to compress the meat, which will toughen it. Shape the mixture into meatballs ½ inch in diameter.

2 Heat enough canola oil to cover the meatballs in a deep sauté pan to a temperature of 375°F. (A drop of water flicked into the oil will sizzle on contact.) Lower the meatballs into the oil and fry them for 3 to 4 minutes, rotating to cook on all sides. Use tongs or a slotted spoon to transfer the meatballs to paper towels to drain.

3 Heat half the olive oil in a large skillet over medium-high heat. Add the onion and sauté until translucent, about 4 minutes. Add the mushrooms, season with salt and pepper, and cook over medium-high heat for 5 minutes. Add the peas, toss, and sauté for 2 to 3 minutes. Add the stock and mint. Cook for another 5 minutes. Taste and, if necessary, adjust the seasoning. Add the meatballs, toss well, and set aside, covered, to keep warm.

4 Bring a large pot of salted water to a boil. Add the pasta and cook until al dente. Reserve about ¼ cup cooking liquid, then drain the pasta and stir it into the sauce. Over very low heat, add the butter and the remaining Parmigiano, and a few tablespoons of the cooking water. Taste and adjust the seasoning and toss thoroughly, drizzling with the rest of the olive oil.

VINO A young, sparkling Prosecco from the Veneto may seem an unusual selection for meatballs, but because these are made with veal, it's the perfect choice here.

PORTOBELLO MUSHROOM AND POTATO LASAGNE

SERVES 6 AS AN APPETIZER OR 4 AS A MAIN COURSE

IL CLASSICO

Traditional Tuscan cuisine contains many layered dishes, not only lasagne (page 18), but cauliflower and bread casseroles, eggplant Parmigiana, and potato gratin, to name just a few.

LA MIA VERSIONE

This recipe is essentially a vegetarian terrine inspired by the textures and contrasts of lasagne and other layered Tuscan classics.

---

1 POUND CELERY ROOT

JUICE OF 1 LEMON

FINE SEA SALT

1 LARGE IDAHO POTATO (ABOUT 1 POUND), PEELED AND SLICED LENGTHWISE ⅛ INCH THICK

¼ CUP EXTRA VIRGIN OLIVE OIL

1 GARLIC CLOVE, PEELED AND CRUSHED

1 POUND PORTOBELLO MUSHROOMS, STEMS REMOVED, CLEANED WITH A DAMP TOWEL, AND SLICED ¼ INCH THICK

LEAVES FROM 1 SMALL BUNCH THYME

FRESHLY GROUND BLACK PEPPER

1 TABLESPOON UNSALTED BUTTER

2 LARGE EGGS

½ CUP HEAVY CREAM

¾ CUP WHOLE MILK

5 OUNCES TALEGGIO CHEESE, CUT INTO SMALL DICE

PINCH OF FRESHLY GRATED NUTMEG

1 Preheat the oven to 325°F.

2 Peel the celery root with a potato peeler and slice it into ⅛-inch-thick slices. Place it in a mixing bowl and add the lemon juice and enough water to cover the slices. (This will keep them from discoloring.)

3 Bring a large pot of salted water to a boil. Add the potato and cook until softened, 5 to 6 minutes.

4 Remove the celery root from the acidulated water, then add it to the boiling salted water with the potato. Cook for 1 to 2 minutes, drain the potato and celery root pieces in a colander, and then place them on a clean towel.

5 Warm the olive oil in a sauté pan over medium heat. Add the garlic and sauté until brown, about 3 minutes. Add the mushrooms and thyme, season to taste with salt and pepper, and cook for 5 minutes.

6 Grease an ovenproof 8-inch-square baking pan with the butter. Place the celery root, potatoes, and mushrooms in the pan, alternating vegetables and overlapping the pieces.

7 Break the eggs into a mixing bowl and add the cream, milk, Taleggio, and nutmeg. Season with salt and pepper and mix well.

8 Pour the egg mixture over the vegetables and place in the preheated oven. Cook until golden on top, about 30 minutes. Remove the pan from the oven and let rest for 10 minutes. Cut into individual portions and serve.

VINO The subtle fruit of a full-bodied Merlot from the Russian River area will round out the qualities of this dish.

Springtime

in Tuscany is a metaphor for one of life's great lessons: you must seize opportunities when they arise, for they may not be there tomorrow. So it is with *vegetali di primavera*, or spring vegetables. When spring comes to Tuscany, culinary opportunities abound. Different vegetables at their peak of youthful perfection—a stage we call *primizie*—turn up every few days. And you must take them when you can, because you might wake up tomorrow to find that they are gone or have lapsed into some inferior state that simply isn't as appealing.

For example, when you see the first fava beans of the year, you should savor as many of them as possible, even if only with a piece of Pecorino Toscano cheese. We usually cook fava beans in the United States, but in Tuscany they're so tender you can eat them raw. The same is true of early peas and asparagus and baby artichokes, which if they are cooked should be barely at all.

Consider the first spring artichokes, with their vibrant purple-green hue that lets you know that all their fresh, sweet flavor needs is a quick swipe in olive oil seasoned with salt and pepper, or a paper-thin slicing with an accompaniment of caciotta cheese to offset their natural essence of licorice.

Or imagine delicate peas so perfect and sweet that you want to enjoy them in as many ways as possible, in a ragout with prosciutto, tossed with fettuccine and onions for a quick pasta dish, or in a light tomato sauce for seafood and veal.

When you make the recipes in this chapter, please do your best to respect the delicacy of the vegetables themselves. Make the lightest pasta you can for that artichoke lasagne. Use a modicum of batter on those fried asparagus. Don't smother the artichoke and potato parmigiana; use just enough cheese to make your point. These are precious ingredients that you may only get one chance with—treat them that way.

It should of course be noted that while they may be a metaphor for life in many ways, spring vegetables do promise one hopeful difference—unlike many of life's passed opportunities, they will come again next year, just as ripe and ready for the taking as they were in years gone by.

FRIED ARTICHOKES AND ASPARAGUS WITH CAPER MAYONNAISE

SERVES 4 AS AN APPETIZER

IL CLASSICO

Fried artichokes or asparagus are a traditional Tuscan accompaniment to roasted meats, especially spring lamb.

LA MIA VERSIONE

This recipe makes these side dishes the center of attention as a stand-alone appetizer.

---

2 LARGE EGGS

2 CUPS CANOLA OIL PLUS ABOUT 1 QUART FOR FRYING VEGETABLES

½ CUP EXTRA VIRGIN OLIVE OIL

JUICE OF 2½ LEMONS

⅓ CUP CAPERS, SQUEEZED OF EXCESS BRINE

FINE SEA SALT

1½ POUNDS ASPARAGUS, TOUGH STEM ENDS SNAPPED OFF

16 BABY ARTICHOKES, THE TOUGHEST OUTSIDE LEAVES REMOVED AND THE TIPS TRIMMED

2 CUPS RICE FLOUR

FRESHLY GROUND BLACK PEPPER

½ CUP LIGHT BEER

¾ CUP DRY WHITE WINE

¾ CUP SPARKLING WATER

1 Make the caper mayonnaise: place the eggs in the bowl of a blender and process while slowly adding 2 cups canola oil, then the olive oil, the juice of 1½ lemons, and the capers, until the capers are coarsely chopped. Season lightly with salt. Set aside.

2 Fill a bowl with ice water and set aside.

3 Blanch the asparagus in boiling salted water for 50 seconds, then place them in the ice water. Remove from the water, drain, and pat them dry.

4 Place the artichokes in a bowl and cover with water and the juice of the remaining lemon.

5 Blanch the artichokes in boiling salted water for 1 minute, then place them in the ice water. Remove from the water, drain, and pat them dry.

6 Place the rice flour in a mixing bowl and make a well in the center. Add 2 teaspoons salt and a pinch of pepper to the well, then pour in the beer, wine, and sparkling water. Mix with a whisk to incorporate all the flour and obtain a homogenous batter with the texture of thin cream.

7 Place the canola oil in a deep frying pan over high heat. When the oil reaches 375°F (a drop of water flicked into the oil will sizzle on contact) or is on the verge of smoking, dip the asparagus and artichokes in the rice flour batter, then add them to the pan

a few at a time and cook until golden, about 3 minutes. Use tongs to transfer them to paper towels to absorb the oil.

8 Serve the fried artichokes and asparagus with the caper mayonnaise.

VINO A crisp, clean New Zealand Sauvignon Blanc will underscore the mineral flavor of the artichokes and the grassy quality of the asparagus.

EGGS COOKED IN A CROCK, SERVED OVER ASPARAGUS PUREE

——————

SERVES 4 AS A BRUNCH MAIN COURSE

IL CLASSICO

Eggs served sunny side up with tomato and Parmigiano-Reggiano cheese is a time-honored spring dish in Tuscany.

LA MIA VERSIONE

This recipe adds asparagus puree to the mix to further the seasonal tone of this classic.

This is delicious as a brunch dish served with toasted brioche slices to soak up the egg and sauce.

1½ POUNDS THIN ASPARAGUS

FINE SEA SALT

¼ CUP EXTRA VIRGIN OLIVE OIL

3 SHALLOTS, MINCED

10 FRESH TARRAGON LEAVES

FRESHLY GROUND BLACK PEPPER

½ CUP VEGETABLE STOCK

¼ CUP OLIVE OIL FOR THE EGGS

8 LARGE EGGS

1 Cut off and set aside the asparagus tips. Trim off the toughest lower part of the asparagus stalks. Peel the rest of the stalks and slice them crosswise into ¼-inch segments. Set aside, separate from the stalks.

2 Fill a bowl with ice water and set it aside.

3 Bring a pot of salted water to a boil. Add the asparagus stems. Blanch them for about 1 minute, then use a slotted spoon to transfer them to the ice water to stop the cooking and preserve their verdant color.

4 Warm half the extra virgin olive oil in a sauté pan set over medium-high heat. Add the shallots and sauté until translucent, 2 to 3 minutes, then add the asparagus stems and the tarragon. Season with salt and pepper, stir, and cook for 2 to 3 minutes. Add the vegetable stock and cook until the asparagus is soft but retains its green hue.

5 Remove the pan from the heat and let its contents cool to a warm temperature. Transfer to the bowl of a blender or food processor fitted with the steel blade. Add the remaining extra virgin olive oil and pulse until it has the consistency of heavy cream.

6 Transfer the asparagus puree to a sauté pan and gently warm it over medium heat.

(continued)

Stir in the asparagus tips and cook for 2 to 3 minutes, until warmed through. Season with salt and pepper, cover, and remove from the heat.

7 Heat the olive oil in a large sauté pan and cook the eggs sunny side up. (You will almost certainly have to do this in 2 batches. Use 2 pans or start with half the oil and add the remaining oil before the second batch.)

8 Divide the puree among 4 plates and place 2 eggs on each plate. Serve at once.

VINO A young Prosecco from Piemonte will cleanse the palate of rich, egg flavor after each bite.

PEAS IN A LIGHT TOMATO SAUCE WITH SCRAMBLED EGGS

SERVES 4 AS AN APPETIZER OR A BRUNCH MAIN COURSE

IL CLASSICO

This recipe is based on the classic uova e pomodoro, in which eggs are scrambled with tomato sauce.

LA MIA VERSIONE

Here, uova e pomodoro is reconceived for spring with the addition of peas and mint.

1 Place the butter and olive oil in a sauté pan over medium-low heat. Add the shallots and sauté until translucent, 6 to 7 minutes, then add the diced tomatoes and season with salt and pepper. Cook for 5 minutes, then stir the peas into the sauce and cook until the peas are tender but still bright green, about 10 minutes.

2 Break the eggs into the pan and stir well and constantly with a wooden spoon. Add the mint and season with salt and pepper. Cook for 1 to 2 minutes, until the eggs are creamy. Divide among 4 plates and serve with warm toasted country bread.

VINO Soave, the most classical wine of the Veneto (especially a young one), is ideal here.

2 TABLESPOONS UNSALTED BUTTER

2 TABLESPOONS EXTRA VIRGIN OLIVE OIL

2 SHALLOTS, CHOPPED

4 VINE-RIPENED TOMATOES, BLANCHED, PEELED, SEEDED, AND CUT INTO ½-INCH DICE (SEE NOTE, PAGE 25)

FINE SEA SALT

FRESHLY GROUND BLACK PEPPER

2 CUPS FRESH PEAS OR A 1-POUND BAG DEFROSTED FROZEN PEAS

8 LARGE EGGS

8 FRESH MINT LEAVES

4 SLICES TOASTED TUSCAN COUNTRY BREAD

BRAISED SQUID WITH PEAS AND TOMATO

———

SERVES 6 AS AN APPETIZER OR 4 AS A MAIN COURSE

IL CLASSICO

A dish cooked in umido is slow-cooked in a scant amount of liquid; calamari in umido is usually fashioned in a very earthy mode, with garlic and tomato dominating the dish.

LA MIA VERSIONE

This is a lighter, gentler variation of calamari in umido, with mint and peas making the greatest impact (and no garlic at all).

¼ CUP EXTRA VIRGIN OLIVE OIL

1 CUP CHOPPED SCALLION, BOTH WHITE AND GREEN PARTS

2½ POUNDS FRESH CALAMARI, CLEANED, RINSED, BODIES CUT INTO ¼-INCH-WIDE SLICES

FINE SEA SALT

FRESHLY GROUND BLACK PEPPER

1 CUP DRY WHITE WINE

4 LARGE VINE-RIPENED TOMATOES, BLANCHED, PEELED, SEEDED, AND CUT INTO ½-INCH DICE (SEE NOTE, PAGE 25)

3 CUPS FRESH SWEET PEAS, OR DEFROSTED FROZEN PEAS

3 TABLESPOONS CHOPPED FRESH FLAT-LEAF PARSLEY

6 FRESH MINT LEAVES, TORN BY HAND

1 In a flameproof casserole, heat the olive oil over medium heat. Add the scallion and sauté until the white part is translucent, about 5 minutes.

2 Add the calamari, season with salt and pepper, and sauté over medium-high heat for 5 minutes.

3 Add the wine; let the wine evaporate, about 3 minutes, then add the diced tomatoes. Cook for 15 more minutes over low heat, then stir in the peas and let simmer for 10 minutes or until the peas are cooked but still bright green. Finish with the parsley and mint. Divide among individual plates and serve at once.

VINO A good Traminer, a white wine from the Trentino region or Austria, is a fine match for this dish.

THREE VARIATIONS ON FAVA BEANS AND PECORINO TOSCANO

IL CLASSICO

One of the most classic of all Tuscan pairings is that of fresh fava beans and fresh Pecorino Toscano cheese, a soft sheep's milk cheese that ripens in the spring. Americans used to blanched fava beans would probably be surprised to see Tuscans peeling favas and devouring them one after another raw. Eaten either in this way, alternating bites of fava and cheese, or in a simple salad drizzled with olive oil, favas and Pecorino are an institution unto themselves.

LA MIA VERSIONE 1

INSALATA DI PECORINO E VERDURE
SPRING VEGETABLE AND PECORINO TOSCANO SALAD

SERVES 6 AS A SALAD

Pecorino Toscano is so closely associated with fava beans that it's easy to overlook its affinity for so many other spring vegetables, in this case artichokes, asparagus, and peas.

JUICE OF 1 LEMON

6 BABY ARTICHOKES, TOUGH OUTER LEAVES REMOVED AND TIPS CUT OFF

FINE SEA SALT

1 BUNCH FRESH ASPARAGUS, TOUGH LOWER PART OF STEMS SNAPPED OFF

12 GARLIC CLOVES

1½ CUPS WHOLE MILK

¼ CUP EXTRA VIRGIN OLIVE OIL

6 ANCHOVIES IN OLIVE OIL, DRAINED

1 CUP SHELLED FRESH FAVA BEANS, PEELED (BLANCHED FIRST FOR EASIER PEELING IF DESIRED)

(continued)

1 CUP FRESH PEAS, BLANCHED FOR 1 MINUTE, THEN DIPPED IN ICE WATER, OR DEFROSTED FROZEN TINY PEAS

1 CUP SHAVED PECORINO TOSCANO

1 Fill a bowl with ice water and stir in the lemon juice.

2 Cut each artichoke into 8 pieces, placing the pieces in the acidulated water.

3 Bring a large pot of salted water to a boil. Drain the artichokes and blanch them in the salted water for 3 minutes. Drain and transfer them to a large cookie sheet to cool.

4 Slice the asparagus into ½-inch diagonal segments. Set the tips aside.

5 Fill a bowl with ice water and set aside.

6 Fill a pot with enough cold water to cover the asparagus pieces. Season with salt and bring the water to a boil over high heat. Add the asparagus segments and blanch for 2 minutes. Add the tips and cook for another 30 seconds, then use a slotted spoon to transfer the asparagus to the ice water to stop the cooking and preserve their color.

7 Place the garlic in a small flameproof casserole and add the milk. Bring the liquid to a boil over high heat, then reduce the heat and simmer until the garlic has fallen apart and has absorbed almost all the milk, about 30 minutes.

8 Warm the olive oil in a small skillet over low heat. Add the anchovies and smash them into a puree with a wooden spoon. Add the garlic-milk mixture and stir vigorously until everything is amalgamated.

9 Place the artichokes in a mixing bowl and add the asparagus, fava beans, and peas. Add the garlic-milk sauce and toss until thoroughly mixed. Top with the shaved Pecorino Toscano and serve family style from the center of the table or divide among salad plates.

VINO Savor a vintage Tuscan Chianti with a classic Tuscan pair: fava and Pecorino.

HOW TO PREPARE AND ENJOY FAVA BEANS

To prepare a fava bean, you must first remove the tough outer pod and then pop each individual fava out of the skin that encases it. One pound of fava beans in the pod yields about ½ cup of beans.

INSALATA DI COCOMERO E FAVE

WATERMELON AND FRESH FAVA BEAN SALAD

———

SERVES 6 AS AN APPETIZER

This recipe adds surprising, sweet watermelon to fava and replaces fresh with aged Pecorino Toscano to offer balance.

6 CUPS WATERMELON IN 1-INCH DICE

2 CUPS SHELLED FRESH FAVA BEANS, PEELED (BLANCHED FIRST FOR EASIER PEELING IF DESIRED), FROM ABOUT 4 POUNDS IN THE POD

1 CUP AGED PECORINO TOSCANO SHAVINGS

½ TEASPOON FINE SEA SALT

FRESHLY GROUND BLACK PEPPER

¼ CUP EXTRA VIRGIN OLIVE OIL

1 Place the watermelon in a salad bowl and add the fava beans and half the Pecorino Toscano. Season with the salt and plenty of pepper, then drizzle with the olive oil. Mix thoroughly.

2 Serve from a salad bowl or divided among 6 salad plates, with the rest of the Pecorino on top.

VINO A soft, young Vernaccia from Tuscany is gentle enough to let these delicate ingredients shine.

ORZOTTO CON FAVE E PECORINO
BARLEY RISOTTO WITH FAVA BEANS AND PECORINO TOSCANO

————

SERVES 6 AS AN APPETIZER OR 4 AS A MAIN COURSE

In addition to how well fava and Pecorino Toscano translate to a warm dish, the other revelation here is how they find each other amid the barley: you'll taste the beans and cheese above all the other ingredients.

1 Warm half the olive oil in a wide heavy saucepan over medium-high heat. Add the onions and sauté until translucent, about 4 minutes.

2 Add the barley, stir well to coat the grains, then add the white wine, stirring continuously to prevent sticking and adding a ladle of stock whenever the liquid has been absorbed. Season to taste with salt and pepper and cook until al dente, about 25 minutes, adding the fava beans after the first 18 minutes.

3 Add the grated Pecorino Toscano, mint leaves, the rest of the olive oil, and the butter, stirring vigorously until the risotto is creamy. To serve, top each portion with Pecorino shavings and a few grinds of black pepper.

VINO A young but full-bodied Nebbiolo from Piemonte will stand up to the hearty barley without overwhelming the fava beans.

⅓ CUP EXTRA VIRGIN OLIVE OIL

8 SPRING ONIONS OR SCALLIONS, FINELY SLICED

3 CUPS BARLEY

1 CUP DRY WHITE WINE

5 CUPS VEGETABLE STOCK, SIMMERING IN A POT ON A BACK BURNER

FINE SEA SALT

FRESHLY GROUND BLACK PEPPER

1½ CUPS SHELLED FRESH FAVA BEANS, PEELED (BLANCHED FIRST FOR EASIER PEELING IF DESIRED), FROM ABOUT 3 POUNDS IN THE POD

1 CUP FRESHLY GRATED AGED PECORINO TOSCANO, PLUS 16 THINLY SHAVED SLICES FOR GARNISH

6 FRESH MINT LEAVES

1 TABLESPOON UNSALTED BUTTER

ARTICHOKE, PANCETTA, AND SCRAMBLED EGG SALAD

SERVES 4 AS AN APPETIZER

IL CLASSICO

Pontormo is a salad of seasonal greens and scrambled eggs. It usually is based on a mesclunlike combination of Boston lettuce, green oak leaf, red oak leaf, and frisée. Occasionally bacon is added for a salty counterpoint.

LA MIA VERSIONE

This recipe uses more substantial artichoke in place of the traditional greens.

JUICE OF 1 LEMON

10 BABY ARTICHOKES

½ CUP FINELY DICED PANCETTA

6 LARGE EGGS, BEATEN

2 CUPS TIGHTLY PACKED FRISÉE

2 TABLESPOONS RED WINE VINEGAR

FINE SEA SALT

¼ CUP EXTRA VIRGIN OLIVE OIL

FRESHLY GROUND BLACK PEPPER

1 Fill a large bowl with cold water and add the lemon juice.

2 Remove the tough outer leaves from the artichokes. Trim off the tips, saving only the tender parts. Cut the artichokes in half lengthwise and then into thin slices, collecting the slices in the bowl of acidulated water as you work.

3 Place the pancetta in a skillet and sauté over low heat until it begins to render its fat. Remove the pancetta from the pan and cover to keep warm. Raise the heat to high, add the eggs to the pan, and cook them as you would scrambled eggs.

4 Place the frisée in a salad bowl and transfer the eggs to the bowl with the frisée.

5 Remove the artichoke slivers from the acidulated water and pat them dry with paper towels. Add them to the salad bowl along with the warm pancetta.

6 In a small bowl, whisk together the vinegar and 1 teaspoon salt. Add the olive oil in a thin stream, continuing to whisk, until a homogenous mixture is formed. Drizzle this over the salad, add a few grinds of black pepper, and toss well. Serve at once.

VINO Serve this with a dry white Lacryma Christi from the Campagna region.

SIX SPRING VEGETABLE CHOPPED SALAD

———

SERVES 6 AS AN APPETIZER

IL CLASSICO

The chopped salad is an American steakhouse staple in which a number of vegetables, usually including tomatoes and onions, are chopped together and dressed with a simple vinaigrette.

LA MIA VERSIONE

This is a chopped salad that celebrates the vegetables of spring: peas, zucchini, fava beans, artichokes, asparagus, and romaine. Be sure to use the freshest vegetables possible, because they will ideally be used raw, as they are in Tuscany.

FINE SEA SALT

4 MEDIUM ZUCCHINI, SLICED LENGTHWISE INTO ⅛-INCH-THICK STRIPS

1½ BUNCHES SMALL ASPARAGUS (ABOUT 15 TOTAL), TIPS TRIMMED OFF AND SET ASIDE SEPARATELY

JUICE OF 1 LEMON

6 BABY ARTICHOKES

1 CUP FRESH PEAS, BLANCHED

1 CUP SHELLED FRESH FAVA BEANS, PEELED (BLANCHED FIRST FOR EASIER PEELING IF DESIRED), FROM ABOUT 2 POUNDS IN THE POD

1 ROMAINE LETTUCE HEART, SLICED CROSSWISE ½ INCH THICK

2 TABLESPOONS RED WINE VINEGAR

1 TEASPOON CHOPPED FRESH MINT

1 TEASPOON CHOPPED FRESH FLAT-LEAF PARSLEY

5 TABLESPOONS EXTRA VIRGIN OLIVE OIL

FRESHLY GROUND BLACK PEPPER

1 Fill a large bowl with ice water and set aside.

2 Bring a pot of salted water to a boil over high heat. Add the zucchini slices and blanch them for 10 seconds. Use tongs or a slotted spoon to transfer the slices to the ice water to stop the cooking and preserve their color. Remove from the ice water, pat them dry with paper towels, and set aside.

3 Add the asparagus to the pot of salted water. Blanch them for about 1 minute, then use tongs or a slotted spoon to transfer them to the ice water to stop the cooking and preserve their color. Remove from the ice water, pat them dry with paper towels, and set aside.

4 Fill a bowl with cold water and add half of the lemon juice.

5 Remove the tough outer leaves from the artichokes. Trim off the tips, saving only the tender parts. Cut the artichokes in half lengthwise and then into thin slices, collecting the slices in the bowl of acidulated water as you work.

6 Add the artichoke slivers to the pot of boiling water and blanch for 10 seconds. Use tongs or a slotted spoon to transfer the slices to the ice water to stop the cooking and preserve their color. Remove from the ice water, pat them dry with paper towels, and set aside.

7 With a very sharp knife, finely chop the asparagus, artichokes, and zucchini, collecting them in a salad bowl as you work. Add the asparagus tips to the bowl last because they are very delicate. Add the peas, fava beans, and romaine.

8 In a small bowl, whisk together the vinegar and 1 teaspoon salt. Continuing to whisk, add the remaining lemon juice, the mint, and the parsley, then add the olive oil in a thin stream, whisking until a homogenous mixture is attained. Drizzle this over the vegetables, season with black pepper, and toss gently. Divide among 6 salad plates and serve.

VINO A light dish requires a light white wine like Vermentina from Cinque Terre, Liguria.

VEGETABLE CARPACCIO WITH PESTO AND PECORINO TOSCANO

―――

SERVES 4 AS AN APPETIZER

IL CLASSICO

Legend has it that carpaccio was created by Harry Cipriani at his legendary bar in Venice. Supposedly designed to suit the carnivorous appetite of a customer who couldn't eat cooked beef, it originally featured a thin slice of raw beef dressed with mayonnaise.

LA MIA VERSIONE

Today, especially in New York City, there are countless variations of carpaccio. This one uses thinly sliced vegetables, topping them with pesto and Pecorino Toscano. The freshness of the ingredients is reinforced by their being sliced paper-thin.

1 LARGE CARROT, PEELED

1 LARGE SEEDLESS CUCUMBER, PEELED

2 MEDIUM ZUCCHINI

FINE SEA SALT

JUICE OF 1 LEMON

1 TABLESPOON PINE NUTS

⅓ CUP EXTRA VIRGIN OLIVE OIL

¼ CUP TIGHTLY PACKED FRESH HERBS SUCH AS FLAT-LEAF PARSLEY, TARRAGON, AND BASIL

FRESHLY GROUND BLACK PEPPER

2 CUPS MESCLUN SALAD

½ CUP COARSELY GRATED PECORINO TOSCANO

1 Slice the carrot, cucumber, and zucchini lengthwise, paper-thin, ideally using a mandoline or slicing machine.

2 Place the carrot, cucumber, and zucchini on a cookie sheet lined with parchment paper. Sprinkle with salt. Let them sit until soft, 2 to 4 hours, then rinse under cool running water and pat them dry between 2 clean kitchen towels.

3 Place the lemon juice, pine nuts, olive oil, and herbs in a blender and season with salt and pepper. Blend until a dressing is formed. If it appears too thick, add 2 tablespoons water. Taste and correct the seasoning if necessary.

4 Arrange the vegetables on a serving platter and drizzle them with three-quarters of the dressing. Toss the mesclun with the remaining dressing and mound in the center of the platter. Scatter one-quarter of the Pecorino over each serving. Serve at room temperature.

VINO Go easy on this dish with a nice, fruity Soave from the Veneto region.

ARTICHOKES STUFFED WITH PROSCIUTTO AND FRESH PEAS

——

SERVES 4 AS AN APPETIZER

IL CLASSICO

This dish has its origins well to the south of Tuscany, in Rome. It is based on carciofi alla Romana (Roman-style artichokes), in which fresh, giant artichokes are rubbed inside and out with a mixture of parsley, mint, and garlic before being cooked gently.

LA MIA VERSIONE

We have enhanced the spring theme of the dish by adding fresh peas and balancing the vegetables with salty prosciutto di Parma.

ARTICHOKES

1 In a small bowl, stir together the parsley, mint, and garlic.

2 Fill a bowl with cold water and add the lemon juice. Trim the artichokes, removing the tough outer leaves and cutting off the top. As you do this, place each artichoke in the acidulated water.

3 Season the artichokes inside and out with salt and pepper. Stuff their cavities with the garlic-herb mixture. Place them upside down in a flameproof casserole large enough to hold them in a single layer without crowding.

4 Pour the olive oil and 2 cups cold water into the casserole, cover with a lid, and place over high heat. Bring to a boil, then lower the heat and simmer for 20 minutes. Remove the casserole from the heat, remove the lid, and set aside at room temperature.

(continued)

¼ CUP CHOPPED FRESH FLAT-LEAF PARSLEY

¼ CUP CHOPPED FRESH MINT

1 GARLIC CLOVE, MINCED

JUICE OF 1 LEMON

8 MEDIUM ARTICHOKES

FINE SEA SALT

FRESHLY GROUND BLACK PEPPER

2 CUPS EXTRA VIRGIN OLIVE OIL

¼ CUP EXTRA VIRGIN OLIVE OIL

8 SCALLIONS, BOTH WHITE AND GREEN PARTS, FINELY SLICED

1 CUP FINELY DICED PROSCIUTTO DI PARMA

3 CUPS FRESH PEAS OR DEFROSTED FROZEN TINY PEAS

¼ TEASPOON SUGAR

FINE SEA SALT

FRESHLY GROUND BLACK PEPPER

½ CUP VEGETABLE STOCK

PEAS

1 Heat the olive oil in a pan. Add the scallions and sauté until the white portion is translucent, 4 to 5 minutes. Add the prosciutto and sauté until the fat is rendered. Stir in the peas, and add the sugar. Season with salt and pepper.

2 Add the stock to the pan and cook over low heat until the peas are tender but retain their bright green color, about 10 minutes.

ASSEMBLY

Stand 2 artichokes up on each of 4 salad plates. Fill each one's cavity with the sweet peas and prosciutto and spoon the remaining peas and prosciutto around the plate.

VINO Enjoy this starter with a very young Frascati, a dry white wine from the Lazio region.

FAVA BEAN AND SCALLOP SOUP

SERVES 6 AS A SOUP

IL CLASSICO

Fava bean soup, a Tuscan springtime staple, is the inspiration for this recipe.

LA MIA VERSIONE

Sweet, tender bay scallops make a perfect complement to the fava beans, especially since they are cooked gently in the soup rather than caramelized in a sauté pan.

APPROXIMATELY ⅓ CUP EXTRA VIRGIN OLIVE OIL

⅓ CUP FINELY DICED PANCETTA

8 SCALLIONS, BOTH WHITE PART AND TENDER GREEN PARTS, VERY THINLY SLICED

1 IDAHO POTATO, PEELED AND VERY FINELY DICED

FINE SEA SALT

FRESHLY GROUND BLACK PEPPER

5 CUPS VEGETABLE STOCK, SIMMERING IN A POT ON A BACK BURNER

2 CUPS SHELLED FRESH FAVA BEANS, PEELED (BLANCHED FIRST FOR EASIER PEELING IF DESIRED), FROM ABOUT 4 POUNDS IN THE POD

1 CUP BAY SCALLOPS

1 HEAD ROMAINE LETTUCE, TOUGH OUTER LEAVES REMOVED AND SLICED CROSSWISE ½ INCH THICK

1 In a deep wide flameproof casserole over medium-high heat, warm enough of the olive oil to coat the bottom. Add the pancetta and sauté until it begins to render its fat.

2 Add the scallions and sauté until the white part is translucent, about 4 minutes. Stir in the potato, season with salt and pepper, and sauté over medium heat for 5 minutes. Pour the hot stock into the casserole and simmer for 15 minutes.

3 Add the fava beans and, when the liquid returns to a boil, add the scallops and romaine lettuce. Simmer for 10 minutes, adjust the seasoning, and finish with the rest of the olive oil. Ladle into individual bowls and serve hot.

VINO You might not usually serve red wine with scallops, but try a young, light-bodied Chianti from Tuscany and see how well it works.

SPLIT PEA AND HAM SOUP, TUSCAN STYLE

SERVES 4 AS A SOUP

IL CLASSICO

Split pea soup, a creamy concoction that finds balance thanks to the addition of cubed ham, is an American favorite.

LA MIA VERSIONE

In this recipe we have "Tuscanized" this soup by making it with prosciutto di Parma instead of ham.

¼ CUP EXTRA VIRGIN OLIVE OIL

1 BUNCH SCALLIONS, BOTH WHITE AND GREEN PARTS, FINELY DICED

¾ CUP PROSCIUTTO DI PARMA IN ¼-INCH DICE

2 CUPS DRIED SPLIT PEAS, RINSED

2 QUARTS VEGETABLE STOCK

FRESHLY GROUND BLACK PEPPER

1 ROMAINE LETTUCE HEART, SLICED CROSSWISE ½ INCH THICK

FINE SEA SALT (OPTIONAL)

1 Warm half of the olive oil in a deep wide flameproof casserole over medium heat. Add the scallions and sauté until translucent, 6 to 7 minutes. Add the prosciutto and cook for 2 to 3 minutes.

2 Add the peas and continue cooking, stirring frequently, until coated. Add enough vegetable stock to cover the peas. Season with black pepper. Simmer for 30 minutes, adding the romaine strips after 25 minutes. Add more stock if the soup dries up or becomes too thick: it should have the texture of cream.

3 Drizzle the soup with the remaining olive oil. Taste and correct the seasoning, adding salt if necessary. Divide among individual bowls and serve.

VINO A very young Montepulciano d'Abruzzo, a sturdy red wine, is a fine counterpart for this hearty soup.

ARTICHOKE AND POTATO PARMESAN

SERVES 4 TO 6 AS AN APPETIZER

IL CLASSICO

Traditionally, Parmigiana refers to vegetables or meat cooked in a single or multiple layers, each one topped with grated Parmesan cheese and mozzarella, which melts when cooked. Frequently the principal ingredient is breaded and fried before being transferred to a casserole and topped with cheese.

LA MIA VERSIONE

This recipe uses two vegetables that are not commonly cooked alla Parmigiana in Italy, artichokes and potatoes. To reinforce the spring theme, Pecorino—the soft young cheese of the season—replaces the Parmesan.

---

2 POUNDS LARGE IDAHO POTATOES

FINE SEA SALT

6 LARGE ARTICHOKES, TOUGH OUTER LEAVES REMOVED AND TIPS CUT OFF

JUICE OF 1 LEMON

¼ CUP PLUS 2 TABLESPOONS EXTRA VIRGIN OLIVE OIL

2 SHALLOTS, FINELY CHOPPED

FRESHLY GROUND BLACK PEPPER

LEAVES FROM 1 SMALL BUNCH FRESH MARJORAM

½ CUP DRY WHITE WINE

1 POUND LARGE VINE-RIPENED TOMATOES

1 TEASPOON SUGAR

8 FRESH BASIL LEAVES, TORN BY HAND

2 GARLIC CLOVES, SLICED

¾ POUND FRESH MOZZARELLA, SLICED ¼ INCH THICK

¾ CUP FRESHLY GRATED PECORINO TOSCANO

1 Preheat the oven to 250°F.

2 Peel the potatoes and slice them ¼ inch thick.

3 Bring a large pot of salted water to a boil over high heat. Add the potatoes and blanch for 5 to 6 minutes. Drain and place on a large cookie sheet lined with a clean towel.

4 Cut each artichoke into 8 slices each and place them in a mixing bowl. Cover with cold water and add the lemon juice.

5 Warm ¼ cup of the olive oil in a sauté pan over medium heat. Add the shallots and sauté until translucent, about 3 minutes. Drain the artichokes and add them to the pan. Season with salt and pepper and add half the marjoram.

6 Sprinkle with the white wine. Let the wine evaporate, about 2 minutes, then remove the pan from the heat.

7 Slice the tomatoes ½ inch thick and place them on a rimmed cookie sheet lined with parchment paper. Place the sugar in a small bowl, add 1 tablespoon salt, and mix well.

(continued)

Sprinkle the sugar-salt mixture on the tomatoes. Add the remaining marjoram, the basil leaves, and the garlic.

8 Place the baking sheet in the oven and cook for 30 minutes. Remove from the oven and set aside to cool.

9 Coat a baking pan with the rest of the olive oil. Arrange the potatoes on the pan in a single layer. Add the artichoke-marjoram mixture as a layer on top of the potatoes. Add the tomatoes as the next layer, then layer on the mozzarella and the Pecorino Toscano.

10 Increase the oven temperature to 300°F. Place the baking pan in the oven and bake for 30 minutes. Remove from the oven, cut into individual portions, and serve.

VINO This dish demands a very rich, full-bodied red wine like a Cabernet from California.

LASAGNE DI PENNE E CARCIOFI AL MASCARPONE

TWO-PASTA LASAGNE WITH ARTICHOKES AND MASCARPONE

———

SERVES 4 AS A MAIN COURSE

IL CLASSICO

Lasagne, with its endless possibilities, is the basis for this recipe as well as several others (pages 18 and 68).

LA MIA VERSIONE

This recipe might put you in mind of the name of one of my restaurants, Coco Pazzo, which means "crazy chef." Who but a crazy chef would use small penne-shaped pasta as part of the filling for a lasagne? But when you think about it, this really isn't that much of a stretch: pasta is, after all, pasta; the penne and lasagne get along just fine. In fact, they nicely contrast each other's texture and mouthfeel.

JUICE OF 1 LEMON

15 BABY ARTICHOKES

¼ CUP PLUS 1 TABLESPOON EXTRA VIRGIN OLIVE OIL

2 LEEKS, VERY THINLY SLICED

FINE SEA SALT

FRESHLY GROUND BLACK PEPPER

¼ CUP DRY WHITE WINE

1 CUP VEGETABLE STOCK, SIMMERING IN A POT ON A BACK BURNER

½ POUND FRESH EGG PASTA SHEETS

½ POUND DRIED PENNETTE PASTA (A SMALLER VERSION OF PENNE)

¾ CUP MASCARPONE

2 TABLESPOONS MINCED FRESH CHIVES

1 TEASPOON PINK PEPPERCORNS, GROUND OR CRUSHED

BUTTER FOR GREASING THE BAKING DISH

½ CUP GRATED PARMIGIANO-REGGIANO

(continued)

1 Fill a bowl with ice water and add the lemon juice. Trim the artichokes, removing the tough outer leaves and cutting off the tips. As you do this, place each artichoke in the acidulated water.

2 Warm ¼ cup of the olive oil in a sauté pan. Add the leeks and sauté them for 1 to 2 minutes. Drain the artichokes, pat them dry with paper towels, and add them to the pan. Season with salt and pepper and sauté for another 2 to 3 minutes. Add the wine and cook until it evaporates—about one minute. Add 2 tablespoons of the vegetable stock and cook for 5 more minutes. Remove from the heat.

3 Transfer a third of the artichoke mixture to a food processor fitted with the steel blade and pulse into a puree. Reserve.

4 Bring a large pot of salted water to a boil over high heat and prepare a large bowl of ice water. Blanch the lasagne sheets in the boiling water, transfer them with tongs to the ice water, then move them to clean towels to dry.

5 In the same boiling water, cook the pennette halfway (about 3 minutes), then drain and place them on a large tray. Drizzle the pasta with the remaining tablespoon olive oil.

6 Warm a sauté pan over low heat. Add the remaining stock and the mascarpone. Stir and add the artichoke puree, chives, and pink pepper. Ladle a quarter of the sauce into a bowl and reserve. Toss the pennette with the sauce that remains in the pan and add the sliced artichokes.

7 Preheat the oven to 325°F.

8 Grease an ovenproof dish with butter and arrange a quarter of the lasagne sheets on the bottom, then add a layer of pennette and sauce. Repeat twice, then sprinkle with the Parmigiano. Finish with another layer of lasagne sheets, pouring the reserved sauce over the top. Bake in the oven for about 30 minutes, then remove, cut into individual portions, and serve.

VINO Enjoy a full-bodied Australian Chardonnay with this white lasagne.

SPRING STEW OF MONKFISH, FAVA BEANS, AND ITALIAN BACON

SERVES 4 AS A MAIN COURSE

IL CLASSICO

Fresh fava bean soup is a free-form Tuscan dish, usually made with rice, that is adapted freely by each cook in his or her own style.

LA MIA VERSIONE

This recipe turns fava bean soup into a meal all its own with the addition of monkfish and a salty counterpoint of diced pancetta.

1¾ POUNDS MONKFISH TAIL, SLICED ½ INCH WIDE

¼ CUP ALL-PURPOSE FLOUR

¼ CUP EXTRA VIRGIN OLIVE OIL

½ CUP PANCETTA IN ¼-INCH DICE

8 SPRING ONIONS OR SCALLIONS, BOTH WHITE AND GREEN PARTS, VERY THINLY SLICED

FINE SEA SALT

FRESHLY GROUND BLACK PEPPER

1 CUP DRY WHITE WINE

2 CUPS SHELLED FRESH FAVA BEANS, PEELED (BLANCHED FIRST FOR EASIER PEELING IF DESIRED), FROM ABOUT 4 POUNDS IN THE POD

2 TO 3 TABLESPOONS VEGETABLE STOCK, IF NEEDED

8 FRESH MINT LEAVES

1 Gingerly dredge the monkfish slices in the flour.

2 Warm the olive oil in a sauté pan over medium heat. Add the pancetta and sauté until the fat is rendered, 4 to 5 minutes. Add the onions and cook until translucent, about 4 minutes.

3 Add the monkfish slices and sauté on both sides until brown, about 4 minutes per side. Season to taste with salt and pepper and sprinkle with the wine. Let the wine evaporate, about 3 minutes, then add the fava beans and cook for 5 minutes; if the mixture appears excessively dry, add the vegetable stock as necessary. Garnish with the mint, divide among 4 dinner plates, and serve.

VINO A full-bodied Merlot from the Sonoma region is a good match for the meaty character of the monkfish.

ROASTED ASPARAGUS AND SPELT OMELET

SERVES 4 AS A BRUNCH MAIN COURSE

IL CLASSICO

If you read about farro, or spelt, which you can do on page 23, you will see that it's commonly used in soups, salads, farrotto, and similar dishes. A highly versatile ingredient, it can be used almost anywhere you would use rice, grains, or legumes.

LA MIA VERSIONE

This recipe stretches the boundaries of spelt applications by using it to add crunch and a distinct rustic flavor to an omelet.

FINE SEA SALT

⅓ CUP SPELT, SOAKED IN COLD WATER FOR 2 HOURS AND DRAINED

4 BUNCHES (ABOUT 10 PER BUNCH) LARGE ASPARAGUS, PEELED, TOUGH LOWER STEM ENDS SNAPPED OFF

¼ CUP EXTRA VIRGIN OLIVE OIL, PLUS MORE FOR COATING THE PAN

FRESHLY GROUND BLACK PEPPER

8 LARGE EGGS

¾ CUP GRATED PARMIGIANO-REGGIANO

1 Preheat the oven to 375°F.

2 Pour enough water into a stockpot to completely immerse the spelt. Season with salt and bring to a boil over high heat. Add the spelt and cook for about 25 minutes, until al dente, then drain it and spread it out on a large cookie sheet to cool.

3 Fill a large bowl with ice water.

4 Fill a large pot with salted water and bring to a boil over high heat. Add the asparagus and blanch for 50 seconds, then use tongs to transfer them to the ice water to stop the cooking and preserve their color. After about a minute, remove them from the water and pat them dry with paper towels.

5 Line a cookie sheet with parchment paper and place the asparagus on it. Brush the spears with the olive oil, season with salt and pepper, and roast for 10 minutes. Remove from the heat and set aside.

6 Break the eggs into a large nonreactive bowl and beat them with a whisk. Add the Parmigiano and cooled spelt and season to taste with salt and pepper.

7 Coat the bottom of a large nonstick ovenproof pan with olive oil and set over medium heat. When the oil is hot, pour in the egg mixture, then cook without stirring for 2 minutes.

(continued)

8 Transfer the pan to the oven and bake until the top is golden brown and the frittata is set, about 20 minutes.

9 Let the frittata cool for 1 minute before removing from the pan. Serve with the roasted asparagus on top.

VINO A good Chilean Merlot will have a nice affinity for the charred flavor of the roasted asparagus.

AUTUMN VEGETABLES

When I think of autumn in Tuscany, I think of weather that goes through a dramatic cycle every twenty-four hours. In a single day you experience cool mornings, a hot—sometimes almost summery—midday, and a cool evening that sends the aroma of the earth swirling around in a romantic darkness that seems to come earlier and earlier. The wind ushered in by the sunset, the mistral that can spark a sense of depression, soon becomes invigorating and reassuring. You begin to feel a desire you haven't had in months: to retreat to the sanctuary of your home, to return to the great smells of your mother's kitchen—and the restorative foods of the season—like roasted beets, turnips, squash, and chestnuts even if you have to create them yourself.

The vegetables of the fall, root vegetables in particular, are among the oldest Tuscan ingredients. They have been in our blood for generations and generations. Like their springtime counterparts, fall vegetables reflect the lives we lead in the season during which we eat them. Just as it becomes too cold for us to spend time in the outdoor air in October and November, so it becomes too cold for vegetables to flourish. Things can't grow on the withering trees—not even leaves—or in the garden. So we turn to the one place where it is warm enough for them to be nurtured: the earth itself.

Fall vegetables are nature's great culinary magic trick. Just when you think her hands are empty, she produces food from the least likely place, as much of it as you like, to last right through the winter.

Everything about food changes in the fall. Even the color of our food changes. No longer do we have the great greens and reds of spring and summer. Instead we are left with the oranges of pumpkins and squashes, the browns of nuts and mushrooms, the deep purple of beets, the soft beiges of potatoes and turnips.

Whereas in the spring and summer we have food that can be devoured raw or after a quick sauté, now we have ingredients that have to be slow-cooked to soften them or draw out their moisture and concentrate their flavor. Yet I find myself nostalgic for fall vegetables every year. In fact it's my favorite time in which to cook and eat.

When the first frost comes, I can't wait for these vegetables that so perfectly suit our circumstances and our appetites. Trapped indoors, with fewer daylight hours, what more soothing activity is there than making a stew or a sauce that needs time on the stove or in the oven? What greater aroma could we ask for than the rich one of roasting garlic and meats wafting through the rooms of our homes? And what greater source of warmth is there than the one that emanates from the burners in our kitchen or from the finished dish itself, filling our stomachs and souls with a food that seems to understand just what we need in these increasingly cold days?

VEGETABLE SOUP FRITTERS

SERVES 6 AS AN APPETIZER

IL CLASSICO

Have you ever wondered what the difference between minestrone and zuppa is? They might seem to be used interchangeably on Italian menus, but here's the distinction: minestrone refers only to vegetable soups. This is one of those cases where recipes vary not just from region to region or even from home to home but actually from day to day in any given home, depending on what's available.

LA MIA VERSIONE

This recipe was inspired by the dense texture of leftover vegetable soup, which can become very thick after a night in the refrigerator.

⅓ CUP EXTRA VIRGIN OLIVE OIL

2 LEEKS, THINLY SLICED

1¼ POUNDS IDAHO POTATOES, PEELED AND CUT INTO ¼-INCH DICE

2 LARGE CARROTS, PEELED AND CUT INTO ¼-INCH DICE

3 CELERY RIBS, CUT INTO ¼-INCH DICE

3 OUNCES BUTTERNUT SQUASH, PEELED AND CUT INTO ¼-INCH DICE

5 OUNCES SAVOY CABBAGE, SLICED INTO ¼-INCH-WIDE STRIPS

¼ POUND (½ BUNCH) SPINACH, STEMS REMOVED

1 CUP DRIED CANNELLINI BEANS, SOAKED OVERNIGHT OR FOR AT LEAST 6 HOURS IN COLD WATER TO COVER

FINE SEA SALT

FRESHLY GROUND BLACK PEPPER

1 QUART VEGETABLE STOCK, SIMMERING IN A POT ON A BACK BURNER

½ POUND ZUCCHINI, PEELED AND CUT INTO ¼-INCH DICE

3 OUNCES ASPARAGUS, TOUGH STEM ENDS REMOVED AND THE REST SLICED ¼ INCH THICK

½ CUP GRATED PARMIGIANO-REGGIANO

½ CUP ALL-PURPOSE FLOUR

1 CUP DRIED BREAD CRUMBS

VEGETABLE OIL, FOR FRYING

1 Warm half the olive oil in a heavy flameproof casserole over medium heat. Add the leeks and sauté until translucent, about 3 minutes.

2 Add the potatoes, carrots, celery, squash, cabbage, spinach, and drained beans. Season with salt and pepper, then add the stock and simmer for 30 minutes.

3 Add the zucchini and asparagus and cook for about 15 more minutes, until the mixture is very thick. Add the rest of the olive oil and the Parmigiano and stir well. Let the soup cool until warm, then refrigerate overnight.

4 The next day, form the mixture into small patties. Turn the flour and bread crumbs out onto a plate and dredge the patties in them.

5 Warm ½ inch of vegetable oil in a deep sauté pan over medium heat until almost smoking. Add the patties and fry them until crisp on both sides, about 1 minute per side. Transfer to paper towels to drain and serve warm.

VINO Serve this with one of the full-bodied, single-estate wines from Tuscany known as the Super Tuscans.

ZUCCHE RIPIENE

STUFFED ACORN SQUASH

—

SERVES 4 AS AN APPETIZER, A SIDE DISH, OR A MAIN COURSE

IL CLASSICO

In Italy the visually dramatic acorn squash is a popular side dish, usually served after it's been split in half and roasted. Occasionally the hollowed-out rind is used as a bowl for a soup made from the squash.

LA MIA VERSIONE

Here we make squash the center of a more complex side dish by filling the scooped-out halves with bread cubes, Fontina, the squash itself, and a touch of cream. It is then baked to create a rich and satisfying side dish to serve with roasted meats or as a vegetarian main course. It's especially delicious with filet mignon.

---

4 SMALL ACORN SQUASH

2 SLICES TUSCAN COUNTRY BREAD, DICED

1 CUP FONTINA VALLE D'AOSTA IN ¼-INCH DICE

FINE SEA SALT

FRESHLY GROUND BLACK PEPPER

1 TEASPOON FRESHLY GRATED NUTMEG

½ CUP HEAVY CREAM

2 TEASPOONS TRUFFLE OIL

ABOUT 4 CUPS KOSHER SALT TO COVER THE BOTTOM OF A BAKING PAN

1 Preheat the oven to 300°F.

2 Cut the top ¾ inch off the squash and set aside. Hollow the squash out with a spoon and cut the pulp into small dice.

3 In a bowl, stir together the bread, Fontina, and squash cubes. Season with salt, pepper, and nutmeg. Toss with the cream and the truffle oil and stuff the squash with this mixture.

4 Line a baking pan with enough coarse salt to cover the bottom to a height of 1 inch. Put the tops back on the stuffed squash and place them on the pan, cover with aluminum foil, and bake for about 40 minutes. Remove the foil and bake for 20 minutes longer.

VINO A dry Pinot Noir from Oregon, the younger the better, will play well off the rich flavors of the Fontina and cream filling.

FRIED BUTTERNUT SQUASH WITH RED WINE VINEGAR AND MINT

SERVES 6 AS AN APPETIZER OR 6 TO 8 AS A SIDE DISH

IL CLASSICO

Cooking something in carpione refers to frying seafood (especially trout, carp, or eel), then preserving it in a marinade. In Tuscany, the technique is sometimes called *scapece,* and mint is often added to expand on the flavor. (Fans of Venetian cuisine will know it as *saor.*)

LA MIA VERSIONE

This recipe applies the principles of carpione to butternut squash, which has a great affinity for all of the flavors, including the mint. It can be served as an appetizer or as an accompaniment to tuna or swordfish.

VEGETABLE OIL TO COAT THE BOTTOM OF A LARGE CASSEROLE

2 POUNDS BUTTERNUT SQUASH, PEELED, SEEDS REMOVED, AND SLICED INTO ¼-INCH-WIDE STRIPS

ALL-PURPOSE FLOUR FOR DUSTING THE BUTTERNUT SQUASH SLICES

FINE SEA SALT

3 TABLESPOONS SUGAR

2 BAY LEAVES

3 GARLIC CLOVES, 1 CLOVE COARSELY CHOPPED

1 CUP RED WINE VINEGAR, PLUS MORE FOR DRIZZLING

½ CUP TIGHTLY PACKED FRESH MINT LEAVES, TORN BY HAND

1 Coat the bottom of a large deep flameproof casserole or skillet with vegetable oil and set over medium-high heat. Lightly dust the squash slices with flour, then place them in the casserole and cook until golden, about 2 minutes per side. Drain them and pat them dry on paper towels. Sprinkle with salt.

2 Pour 1½ cups water into a small skillet over moderate heat and add the sugar, bay leaves, and whole garlic cloves. Cook, stirring, until the sugar starts to caramelize, about 10 minutes. Reduce the heat to very low and carefully add the vinegar, stirring until all the sugar is dissolved. Remove from the heat.

3 Arrange the squash slices on a serving platter. Drizzle with the vinegar and sprinkle the chopped garlic and the mint on top. Cover with plastic wrap and refrigerate overnight. Serve at room temperature.

VINO A full-bodied Chianti Reserve will marry well with the starchy squash.

INSALATA DI VERDURE AUTUNNALI ARROSTE

ROASTED AUTUMN VEGETABLE SALAD

SERVES 4 AS A MAIN COURSE OR 8 AS A SIDE DISH

IL CLASSICO

Roasted vegetables are a popular side dish in Tuscan cooking, as they are all over the world, especially in the fall, when the slow cooking removes moisture from the vegetables, concentrating their flavor.

LA MIA VERSIONE

In this recipe we make roasted vegetables the focus of a salad. The recipe is also noteworthy for the milk-based dressing. Serve this with roasted meats, game, or poultry.

1 Preheat the oven to 300°F.

2 You will need 4 cookie sheets for the following step; if you don't have enough, cook the vegetables in batches: place each diced vegetable (squash, celery root, sweet potato, and turnip) on a separate cookie sheet lined with parchment paper. Toss each with 2 tablespoons of the olive oil and season with salt and pepper to taste. Scatter the rosemary and sage on top of each. Sprinkle the butternut squash with the brown sugar and cover all the pans with aluminum foil.

3 Fill a roasting pan with enough coarse salt to cover the bottom to a depth of 1 inch. Arrange the unpeeled onions on it and cover with aluminum foil.

4 Place the sheet pans in the preheated oven for 25 minutes, then remove all the aluminum foil except for that covering the onions. Cook the butternut squash for 10 more minutes, until gold and caramelized; cook the rest of the vegetables for 25 more minutes, until lightly brown and tender.

5 Remove the pans from the oven and set aside to cool down, then peel the onions and cut them into wedges. Mix all the vegetables in a large bowl.

6 Place the garlic in a small saucepan and add the milk. Place over high heat and bring to a boil. Lower the heat and simmer slowly until the garlic has fallen apart and the liquid has a thin, creamy consistency, about 10 minutes.

2 CUPS PEELED AND SEEDED BUTTERNUT SQUASH IN 1-INCH DICE

2 CUPS PEELED CELERY ROOT IN 1-INCH DICE

2 CUPS PEELED SWEET POTATO IN 1-INCH DICE

2 CUPS PEELED TURNIP IN 1-INCH DICE

½ CUP PLUS 1 TABLESPOON EXTRA VIRGIN OLIVE OIL

FINE SEA SALT

FRESHLY GROUND BLACK PEPPER

8 FRESH ROSEMARY SPRIGS

16 FRESH SAGE LEAVES

1 TABLESPOON LIGHT BROWN SUGAR

2 CUPS KOSHER SALT TO COAT A PAN

2 ONIONS

½ CUP GARLIC CLOVES, PEELED

2 CUPS WHOLE MILK

2 TEASPOONS DIJON MUSTARD

LEAVES FROM 4 FRESH THYME SPRIGS

7 Place the mixture in a blender and add the mustard, thyme, and remaining table-spoon of olive oil.

8 Season with salt and pepper and pulse for 30 seconds.

9 Pour the sauce over the vegetables. Mix thoroughly. Add salt and pepper if necessary, and serve.

VINO A young, fresh Dolcetto from Piemonte is just the thing to accompany the roasted vegetables.

TURNIP AND BEET CARPACCIO WITH GORGONZOLA

——

SERVES 4 AS AN APPETIZER

IL CLASSICO

Like the recipe featured on page 88, this dish was inspired by carpaccio, the famous dish created by Harry Cipriani at his Venice bar that featured paper-thin slices of raw beef.

LA MIA VERSIONE

Like many New York restaurateurs and chefs, I have enjoyed experimenting with the carpaccio format over the years, here using it as an unusual way to plate roasted vegetables. Though carpaccio traditionally implies "raw," I use it here to suggest something cooked, then served cooled and sliced paper-thin.

2 MEDIUM TURNIPS

2 MEDIUM RED BEETS

⅓ CUP GORGONZOLA

½ CUP WHOLE MILK

2 TABLESPOONS WHITE WINE VINEGAR

1 SHALLOT, FINELY MINCED

¼ CUP ROUGHLY CHOPPED WALNUT HALVES

1 Preheat the oven to 350°F.

2 Wrap the turnips and beets in aluminum foil, place on a baking pan, and bake for about 1 hour or until tender when pricked with a toothpick. Remove from the oven, carefully remove the foil, and let them cool.

3 Place the Gorgonzola in a food processor fitted with the plastic paddle. Add the milk, vinegar, and shallot. Process for a few minutes, until the sauce is creamy. If the sauce appears too thick, add a small quantity of milk.

4 Use a mandoline or a food processor to slice the turnips and beets ⅛ inch thick and arrange them alternately on a serving platter or on individual plates. Pour the sauce on top, then finish with the walnuts.

VINO Serve this with a young California Syrah.

ZUCCHINI IN TAGLIO CON POMODORO E BASILICO

SPAGHETTI SQUASH WITH TOMATO, OLIVE OIL, AND BASIL

———

SERVES 4 AS AN APPETIZER

IL CLASSICO

Spaghetti pomodoro e basilico is one of the most famous pasta dishes, renowned even today for how the fragrant basil perfectly balances the sweetness of the tomatoes.

LA MIA VERSIONE

Spaghetti pomodoro e basilico is a late-summer dish, because that's when tomatoes are at their peak. But this recipe turns the combination into a fall surprise by substituting the stringy pulp of spaghetti squash for the pasta from which it takes its name.

2 LARGE SPAGHETTI SQUASH, HALVED

4 CUPS CHERRY TOMATOES, HALVED

3 TEASPOONS FINE SEA SALT MIXED WITH 1 TEASPOON SUGAR

20 FRESH BASIL LEAVES

2 FRESH ROSEMARY SPRIGS

4 FRESH THYME SPRIGS

4 MEDIUM VINE-RIPENED TOMATOES

1 TEASPOON FINE SEA SALT OR TO TASTE

FRESHLY GROUND BLACK PEPPER

3 TABLESPOONS EXTRA VIRGIN OLIVE OIL

½ CUP SHAVED PECORINO ROMANO

1 Preheat the oven to 250°F.

2 Pour a few cups of water into a pot and bring to a boil over high heat. Place the squash in a steamer basket and place over the boiling water. Steam, covered, for about 15 minutes, until softened. Use a fork to remove the pulp from the squash. It should resemble long, spaghetti-like strands. Set aside.

3 Place the cherry tomatoes cut side up on a sheet pan lined with parchment paper. Sprinkle with the salt-sugar mixture, then add 10 basil leaves, tearing them by hand as you do. Scatter the rosemary and thyme sprigs over the tomatoes and bake for about 40 minutes, until dry but not shriveled.

4 Set a large pot of water over high heat and bring to a boil. Add the vine-ripened tomatoes and cook for 1 minute, then use tongs to transfer them to a bowl of ice water. Once cool, peel them with the aid of a paring knife (the skin should come right off). Cut them into ¾-inch dice, seeding them as you work.

5 Place the oven-dried cherry tomatoes in a mixing bowl and add the spaghetti squash, diced tomatoes, and remaining basil leaves, torn by hand just before placing them in the bowl. Season with the salt and pepper and drizzle with the olive oil.

(continued)

6 Divide the contents of the bowl among 4 plates and top each portion with shaved Pecorino Romano. Serve at once.

VINO Have you ever tried a Sauvignon Blanc from Chile? This is the time to do so.

INSALATA DI TREVIGIANO E ENDIVIA CON NOCI E CASTAGNE

RADICCHIO TREVIGIANO SALAD WITH ENDIVE, CHESTNUTS, AND WALNUTS

———

SERVES 4 AS AN APPETIZER

IL CLASSICO

Classically, radicchio Trevigiano is braised or grilled and served on its own as an appetizer or as a vegetable side dish (contorno). Or it is braised, chopped, and served with rice or pasta.

LA MIA VERSIONE

Here radicchio Trevigiano is treated as a salad green, bringing its beautiful color and elegant shape to an unconventional context. If you can't get your hands on a pomegranate, leave it out.

1 Cut the pomegranate in half and pick apart the seeds, removing all the membranes. Squeeze half of the seeds in a potato ricer, reserving the juice.

2 Pour the pomegranate juice into a mixing bowl, then add the lemon juice, salt, and pepper. Whisk and add the olive oil gradually in a thin stream, continuing to whisk until emulsified.

3 Place the radicchio in a salad bowl and add the endive, walnuts, chestnuts, and pomegranate seeds. Toss with the vinaigrette. Divide among 4 individual plates and serve at once.

VINO Try Gattinara, a very original wine from the Marche region of Italy, with this recipe.

1 POMEGRANATE

JUICE OF ½ LEMON

1 TEASPOON FINE SEA SALT

PINCH OF FRESHLY GROUND BLACK PEPPER

¼ CUP EXTRA VIRGIN OLIVE OIL

2 HEADS YOUNG RADICCHIO TREVIGIANO, LEAVES SEPARATED AND SLICED INTO ½-INCH-WIDE STRIPS

2 HEADS BELGIAN ENDIVE, LEAVES SEPARATED AND SLICED INTO ½-INCH-WIDE STRIPS

20 WALNUT HALVES

20 FROZEN CHESTNUTS, DEFROSTED AND PEELED

BUTTERNUT SQUASH, CHESTNUT, AND BLACK CABBAGE SOUP

SERVES 6 AS A SOUP

IL CLASSICO

This recipe was inspired by the cacciucco di funghi described on page 56.

LA MIA VERSIONE

This recipe makes mushrooms a supporting ingredient to the high-impact autumnal squash and chestnuts.

APPROXIMATELY ½ CUP EXTRA VIRGIN OLIVE OIL

4 LEEKS, RINSED AND THINLY SLICED

2 LARGE IDAHO POTATOES, CUT INTO ½-INCH DICE

3 CUPS PEELED AND SEEDED BUTTERNUT SQUASH IN ½-INCH DICE

3 CUPS BLACK CABBAGE OR KALE, SLICED ½ INCH WIDE

FINE SEA SALT

FRESHLY GROUND BLACK PEPPER

3 CUPS MIXED FRESH MUSHROOMS (WHATEVER IS AVAILABLE), QUARTERED

2 CUPS FROZEN CHESTNUTS, DEFROSTED AND PEELED

2 GARLIC CLOVES, MINCED

¼ CUP FRESHLY GRATED PARMIGIANO-REGGIANO

1 Pour enough of the olive oil into a flameproof casserole to cover its bottom and set the casserole over medium heat. Add the leeks and sauté them until translucent, about 3 minutes.

2 Add the potatoes and cook them for 6 to 7 minutes. Add the squash and cabbage and season with salt and pepper. Cover with boiling water, then cook for another 20 minutes.

3 Add the mushrooms and chestnuts. Taste to adjust the seasoning. Cook for 20 more minutes, then add the minced garlic and the rest of the olive oil and season with black pepper.

4 To serve, divide the soup among individual bowls and top each serving with the grated Parmigiano.

VINO Earthy soups call for a good-vintage Brunello di Montalcino from Tuscany.

PAPPARDELLE WITH ROASTED BUTTERNUT SQUASH, CRUMBLED SWEET SAUSAGE, AND SAGE

SERVES 6 AS AN APPETIZER OR 4 AS A MAIN COURSE

IL CLASSICO

Squash, sage, and sausage is the defining combination of minestra di zucca, a classic pumpkin soup.

LA MIA VERSIONE

The players in this soup have been recast as the ingredients of an unusual pasta that pairs sweet with sweet (squash and sausage), as opposed to the bitter accompaniment you might expect. The sage infuses the dish with a woodsy flavor.

1 Preheat the oven to 250°F.

2 Place three-quarters of the butternut squash in a bowl. Add the bay leaves, garlic, 4 of the sage leaves, the brown sugar, and 4 tablespoons of the olive oil and season to taste with salt and pepper. Toss until well mixed.

3 Spread the mixture on a rimmed cookie sheet lined with parchment paper and bake for about 40 minutes, until golden and caramelized.

4 Warm a nonstick sauté pan over medium heat. Add the sausage and cook until the fat is rendered. Drain off the fat, then add the wine and let it evaporate, about 2 minutes.

5 Warm 2 tablespoons of the remaining olive oil in a sauté pan over medium heat. Add half the leek and sauté until wilted, about 2 minutes. Add the rest of the butternut squash and season with salt and pepper. Add the stock and cook until the squash is soft, about 25 minutes. Remove from the heat.

6 When the squash mixture has cooled to just warm, process it in a blender to make a thin sauce.

(continued)

2 POUNDS BUTTERNUT SQUASH PULP, CUT INTO ¾-INCH DICE (FROM A 3-POUND SQUASH)

2 BAY LEAVES

3 GARLIC CLOVES

10 SAGE LEAVES

1 TABLESPOON LIGHT BROWN SUGAR

½ CUP EXTRA VIRGIN OLIVE OIL

FINE SEA SALT

FRESHLY GROUND BLACK PEPPER

1 CUP CRUMBLED SWEET SAUSAGE

½ CUP DRY WHITE WINE

½ CUP RINSED AND FINELY SLICED LEEK, WHITE AND LIGHT GREEN PARTS

¾ CUP VEGETABLE STOCK

1 POUND FRESH PAPPARDELLE

⅓ CUP FRESHLY GRATED PARMIGIANO-REGGIANO

7 Warm the remaining olive oil in a sauté pan large enough to hold the pasta. Add the remaining leek and sauté until translucent, about 3 minutes. Add the sausage, remaining sage leaves, and roasted butternut squash and cook for 5 minutes. Add the sauce, stirring well, and simmer for 5 more minutes.

8 Bring a large pot of salted water to a boil. Add the pappardelle and cook until al dente. Drain the pasta and add to the large sauté pan, mixing thoroughly. Sprinkle with the Parmigiano.

9 Divide the pasta and sauce among individual plates and serve at once.

VINO Try this with Sfurzat, an unusual red wine from the north of Italy.

BEET FETTUCCINE WITH LAMB SAUCE

———

SERVES 6 AS AN APPETIZER OR 4 AS A PASTA

IL CLASSICO

Lamb sauce is one of the most popular sauces in Tuscany. Often it begins life as lamb stew, which is then ground up the next day to make a pasta sauce.

LA MIA VERSIONE

This recipe goes right to the second stage mentioned above, making a lamb pasta sauce. The sweetness of beets is a perfect foil for the flavor of lamb, and capturing the flavor (and color) of beets in a pasta is a novel way to bring them to the table.

---

2 CUPS DURUM FLOUR (SEE IN SEARCH OF . . . , PAGE 16) OR ALL-PURPOSE FLOUR

3 LARGE EGGS

2 OUNCES RED BEET, ROASTED FOR 30 MINUTES, COOLED, PEELED, PUREED, AND SQUEEZED IN CHEESECLOTH TO REMOVE AS MUCH MOISTURE AS POSSIBLE

½ TEASPOON FRESHLY GRATED NUTMEG

¾ CUP FRESHLY GRATED PARMIGIANO-REGGIANO OR PECORINO ROMANO

SEMOLINA FLOUR FOR DUSTING A SHEET PAN

APPROXIMATELY ⅓ CUP EXTRA VIRGIN OLIVE OIL

½ CUP CHOPPED SHALLOT

¼ CUP CHOPPED CARROT

¼ CUP CHOPPED CELERY

2 CUPS BONELESS LAMB FROM THE SHOULDER OR LEG, CUT INTO ½-INCH DICE

FINE SEA SALT

FRESHLY GROUND BLACK PEPPER

2 TABLESPOONS RED WINE VINEGAR

1 CUP RED WINE

1 CUP VEAL OR CHICKEN STOCK

1 HERB SACHET: 2 GARLIC CLOVES, 1 BAY LEAF, 4 CRUSHED JUNIPER BERRIES, AND 5 PEPPERCORNS TIED IN A CHEESECLOTH BUNDLE

(continued)

1 CUP PEELED FROZEN CHESTNUTS OR CHESTNUTS IN NATURAL JUICE

2 CUPS PEELED BUTTERNUT SQUASH IN ½-INCH DICE

1 FRESH ROSEMARY SPRIG

1 FRESH THYME SPRIG

1 GARLIC CLOVE

2 TEASPOONS LIGHT BROWN SUGAR

1 Place the flour on a smooth, clean surface and make a well in the middle. Place the eggs, beet puree, nutmeg, and ½ cup Parmigiano in the well and mix them into the flour a little at a time with the help of a fork. Knead until the dough has a smooth and even consistency.

2 Roll the dough through a pasta machine to make thin sheets about ⅛ inch thick. Dust a rimmed cookie sheet with semolina flour, then pass the dough sheets through the pasta machine attachment for fettuccine and spread them out on the pan.

3 Pour enough of the olive oil into a flameproof casserole to cover the bottom and warm it over medium heat. Add the shallot, carrot, and celery and lower the heat to low. Sauté until the shallot is translucent, about 5 minutes.

4 In the meantime, pour enough of the remaining olive oil into a wide deep skillet to cover the bottom and set over medium-high heat. Add the lamb and sear it while seasoning with salt and pepper, 3 to 5 minutes.

5 Add the meat to the vegetables and mix well. Cook for 5 minutes, then deglaze first with the vinegar, then with the wine. Let evaporate, then add the veal stock and the herb sachet, stirring well. Season with salt and pepper and simmer until the meat is soft and the sauce reduced, 30 to 40 minutes; after 20 minutes, add the chestnuts and let them simmer as well. If the sauce dries up, add a little bit of water.

6 In the meantime, place the squash in a mixing bowl and add the rosemary, thyme, garlic, brown sugar, and 1 tablespoon of the remaining olive oil. Season with salt and pepper, then place on a baking sheet and roast in the preheated oven for about 25 minutes, until soft but still firm.

(continued)

7 Add the squash mixture to the sauce and cook together for 5 minutes.

8 Set a large pot of salted water over high heat and bring to a boil. Add the fettuccine and cook until al dente, 2 to 3 minutes.

9 Add the pasta to the sauce and mix thoroughly. Serve with remaining Parmigiano sprinkled on top.

VINO I suggest Barbaresco, a very complex red wine from Piemonte, to go with this complex pasta.

FETTUCCINE WITH AUTUMN VEGETABLE SAUCE

SERVES 6 AS AN APPETIZER OR 4 AS A PASTA

IL CLASSICO

Caponata di vegetali is a Tuscan stew of late-summer vegetables simmered together in olive oil and garlic.

LA MIA VERSIONE

By slow-cooking some autumn vegetables until they soften enough to be used in a sauce, we create an unusual way to savor the flavors of the fall—sort of an autumn ratatouille—and to get more kinds of them on one plate than is usually possible.

---

2 CUPS DURUM FLOUR (SEE IN SEARCH OF . . . , PAGE 16) OR ALL-PURPOSE FLOUR

3 LARGE EGGS

2 OUNCES RED BEET, ROASTED FOR 30 MINUTES, COOLED, PEELED, PUREED, AND SQUEEZED THROUGH CHEESECLOTH TO REMOVE AS MUCH MOISTURE AS POSSIBLE

¼ TEASPOON FRESHLY GRATED NUTMEG

¼ CUP FRESHLY GRATED PARMIGIANO-REGGIANO, PLUS EXTRA FOR TOSSING WITH THE PASTA

SEMOLINA FLOUR FOR DUSTING A COOKIE SHEET

1 CUP PEELED CELERY ROOT IN ¾-INCH DICE

1 CUP PEELED TURNIP IN ¾-INCH DICE

⅓ CUP EXTRA VIRGIN OLIVE OIL

LEAVES FROM 2 FRESH ROSEMARY SPRIGS, 1 TEASPOON CHOPPED, THE REST LEFT WHOLE

FINE SEA SALT

FRESHLY GROUND BLACK PEPPER

1 CUP FROZEN CHESTNUTS, BLANCHED AND PEELED

1 TEASPOON LIGHT BROWN SUGAR

2 BAY LEAVES

½ CUP RINSED CHOPPED LEEK, WHITE AND GREEN PARTS

(continued)

1 Preheat the oven to 300°F.

2 Place the flour on a smooth, clean surface and make a well in the middle. Place the eggs, beet puree, nutmeg, and Parmigiano in the well and mix them into the flour a little at a time with the help of a fork. Knead until the dough has a smooth and even consistency.

3 Roll the dough through a pasta machine to make sheets about ⅛ inch thick. Dust a sheet pan with semolina flour, then pass the dough sheets through the pasta machine attachment for fettuccine and spread them out on the pan.

4 Place half the celery root in each of 2 baking dishes. Add half the turnip, 1 table-spoon of the olive oil, and 1 teaspoon rosemary leaves to each dish, and season both with salt and pepper. Mix well and cover with aluminum foil, then roast for about 20 minutes, until soft. Remove the foil and roast until golden brown, about 10 more minutes.

5 Place the chestnuts in a mixing bowl and add the brown sugar, 1½ teaspoons olive oil, 1 teaspoon rosemary leaves, and the bay leaves and season with salt and pepper. Roast them uncovered for about 10 minutes, until lightly caramelized.

6 Set aside 2 tablespoons of the remaining olive oil and pour the rest into a sauté pan over low heat. Add the leek and sauté until translucent, about 2 minutes. Season to taste with salt and pepper, then add all the celery root, turnip, and chestnuts. Mix thoroughly and cook for 5 minutes.

7 Bring a large pot of salted water to a boil. Add the fettuccine and cook until al dente, no more than 3 minutes.

8 Add the pasta to the sauce and mix well. Add the chopped rosemary leaves and the Parmigiano, then mix well, adding a little bit of cooking liquid if the pasta seems too dry. Drizzle with the reserved olive oil.

VINO Serve this autumn pasta with a wine made for fall: a full-bodied Zinfandel from California.

GNOCCHI INTEGRALI CON CICORIA E PECORINO

WHOLE WHEAT GNOCCHI WITH DANDELION GREENS AND PECORINO

SERVES 6 AS AN APPETIZER OR 4 AS A PASTA

IL CLASSICO

Gnocchi are little pasta dumplings traditionally made with semolina flour and potato.

LA MIA VERSIONE

Whole wheat gnocchi is a thoroughly modern concept that provides a hearty contrast to the accompaniments of dandelion greens and Pecorino cheese. Not only does it taste more complex than traditional gnocchi, but the light brown color looks more attractive here as well.

1 Bring a large pot of salted water to a boil over high heat. Add the unpeeled potatoes and cook until tender but not falling apart.

2 Drain the potatoes, then peel them and pass them through a food mill or mash with a masher (don't use a food processor; they'll become gluey). Transfer the potatoes to a clean work surface. Make a well in the center and add the 2 flours, baking powder, egg, and Parmigiano. Season with salt and black pepper, then mix well until you have a homogenous dough.

3 Knead the dough until smooth; if too sticky, add a little more flour. Divide the dough into 4 portions and roll each into a ½-inch-wide log. Dust a jelly-roll pan with flour, then cut the logs into 1-inch pieces, placing the gnocchi pieces on the pan as you cut them.

4 Warm half the olive oil in a wide sauté pan over medium-high heat. Add the garlic, red pepper, and greens, then season to taste with salt and add 1 tablespoon water. Cover, reduce the heat, and braise the greens for about 20 minutes.

5 Bring a large pot of salted water to a boil over high heat. Add the gnocchi and cook until they float, about 3 minutes. *(continued)*

FINE SEA SALT

1½ POUNDS IDAHO POTATOES

1 CUP ALL-PURPOSE FLOUR, PLUS MORE FOR DUSTING A JELLY-ROLL PAN

1 CUP WHOLE WHEAT FLOUR, PLUS MORE IF NECESSARY

PINCH OF BAKING POWDER

1 LARGE EGG

1¼ CUPS GRATED PARMIGIANO-REGGIANO

FRESHLY GROUND BLACK PEPPER

½ CUP EXTRA VIRGIN OLIVE OIL

2 GARLIC CLOVES, CHOPPED

PINCH OF HOT RED PEPPER FLAKES

2 POUNDS DANDELION GREENS, TOUGHEST LEAVES REMOVED, SLICED 1 INCH WIDE, RINSED, AND SPUN DRY

½ CUP FRESHLY GRATED PECORINO ROMANO

6 Gently remove the gnocchi from the pot with a slotted spoon, reserving the cooking water. Add the gnocchi to the dandelion green mixture, stirring well. Add half the Pecorino and the rest of the olive oil and mix thoroughly. If the dish seems too dry, add some of the gnocchi cooking water.

7 Serve with the rest of the Pecorino on top.

VINO A full-bodied California Zinfandel will harmonize with the peppery dandelion greens.

FISH AND SHELLFISH

To a modern-day Tuscan, water means exploration, just as it did to his ancestors. When we think of the ocean, we think of the great explorers and of Italians leaving native shores for the New World on a steamer ship, which happens to be the image that adorns the menu at Centolire, my New York City restaurant inspired by the Italian-American immigrant experience.

To a well-traveled Tuscan, seafood also signifies exploration—more than any other category of food. Fish and shellfish are synonymous with exploration because they are the ultimate regional foods. Today, as in days gone by, you tend to see the same fruits and vegetables in every region of Italy, as well as meats, poultry, and game. But fish and shellfish vary widely, depending on such factors as whether the water is warm or cold, fresh or salt, and confined to sea or stream. So, specialties from the South are different from specialties from the North and so on. This is true in every large country in the world.

There's another reason that fish and shellfish tend to be best known in their immediate region—because they're so perishable they don't travel well very far. Even with today's speed-of-light shipping possibilities, there are a number of fish and shellfish popular in Italy that are unknown to American diners and enormously popular creatures from American waters that are just as unknown in Italy.

I've always been comfortable exploring new seafood because I had the luxury of growing up in a family of fishermen. My mother's father and brothers made their livings catching and selling eel, crab, sardines, anchovies, mackerel, and other fish and shellfish. And my mother cooked them all in her own distinct way, shaping my palate for years to come. I still smell the aromas of her Tuscan kitchen when I prepare seafood in my own American kitchen today.

This chapter doesn't depend on seasonality for its inspiration. It simply takes its cue from the seafood of different regions and countries, putting a modern spin on Tuscan classics and a Tuscan spin on the fish and shellfish from the United States. From the former group we have calamari stuffed with tentacles, lemon zest, spelt, and onions. From the latter group we have soft-shell crabs, which I never ate until arriving in the United States; red snapper cooked in a clam sauce; and broiled lobster—an American favorite—with Tuscan breading.

There is also a cioppino, a seafood stew popularized by Italian immigrants in San Francisco. (The name, you might notice, sounds similar to cacciucco.) The recipe in this chapter is for the dish we serve at my restaurant Centolire, which tops this dish with a bread crust, putting an age-old Tuscan spin on a New World version of another Tuscan classic.

SAFFRON RICE TIMBALE WITH SEAFOOD SAUCE

SERVES 12 AS AN APPETIZER OR 8 AS A MAIN COURSE

IL CLASSICO

Timballo di pasta is a southern Italian dish in which short pasta and various supporting ingredients are molded into a dome shape and served as a side dish.

LA MIA VERSIONE

This recipe combines the idea of a timbale with a popular Roman dish, supplí (saffron rice balls), then adds a logical shellfish sauce. For extra flavor, top each serving with crumbled toasted walnuts.

SEAFOOD SAUCE

½ CUP EXTRA VIRGIN OLIVE OIL

5 GARLIC CLOVES, CHOPPED

50 MEDIUM MUSSELS, BEARDED AND SCRUBBED

50 LITTLENECK CLAMS OR COCKLES, SCRUBBED AND RINSED

1½ CUPS DRY WHITE WINE

2 PINCHES OF HOT RED PEPPER FLAKES

1 POUND BAY SCALLOPS

2 POUNDS MEDIUM SHRIMP, SHELLED AND DEVEINED

10 RIPE PLUM TOMATOES, PEELED, SEEDED, AND DICED (SEE NOTE, PAGE 25)

¼ CUP CHOPPED FRESH FLAT-LEAF PARSLEY

1 Pour half the olive oil into a wide shallow pan and heat it over medium heat until the oil is almost smoking. Add half the garlic and cook until golden, about 1 minute.

2 Add the mussels and clams, cover, raise the heat to high, and cook until the shells have opened, 4 to 5 minutes. Add half the wine and cook, uncovered, until the alcohol has evaporated, about 4 minutes. Remove from the heat and, when cool enough to handle, remove the mussel and clam shells, reserving 15 of each for garnish and discarding the rest.

3 In the cleaned pan, warm the remaining olive oil over medium heat. Add the remaining garlic and the red pepper and cook until the garlic turns golden, about 1 minute. Add the scallops and shrimp and cook, stirring frequently, until just cooked through, 2 to 3 minutes. Add the remaining wine and continue cooking until the alcohol evaporates, about 3 minutes. Add the tomatoes, clams, and mussels and cook for 5 minutes. Stir in the parsley and remove from the heat.

(continued)

9 CUPS VEGETABLE OR FISH STOCK

FINE SEA SALT

FRESHLY GROUND BLACK PEPPER

2 PINCHES OF SAFFRON THREADS

3 CUPS ARBORIO, CARNAROLI, OR VIALONE
NANO RICE

3 LARGE EGGS, BEATEN

½ CUP GRATED PARMIGIANO-REGGIANO

2 TABLESPOONS UNSALTED BUTTER

1 CUP DRIED BREAD CRUMBS

1 Pour the stock into a 4-quart flameproof casserole and bring to a boil over medium-high heat. Season with salt and pepper and add the saffron. Add the rice, give it a good stir, and cook it until about half done, 10 minutes. Strain the rice and transfer it to a bowl. Let it cool to warm, then stir in the eggs and Parmigiano.

2 Preheat the oven to 375°F.

3 Grease a 10-cup zuccotto or dome mold with butter and coat it with the bread crumbs. Spoon some rice into the casserole and pat it down to form a 1-inch-thick layer on the bottom that continues 3 inches up the sides of the mold.

4 Spoon half the seafood sauce over the rice and cover it with enough rice so that you cannot see any of the sauce. Add enough rice to come almost to the top of the mold. Carefully spoon the remaining sauce over this rice and cover it with all the remaining rice, smoothing it over with a spatula. Cover with aluminum foil.

5 Bake the mold for 40 to 45 minutes. Remove from the oven and remove the foil. Carefully unmold the timbale by placing a large plate or platter over it, inverting the two together, and removing the mold. Garnish with the reserved mussel and clam shells and immediately present at the table.

VINO A very rich, dense dish such as timballo, especially one with shellfish, mingles well with a well-rounded young Chardonnay from Australia. Why a young one? Less woody flavor.

SEAFOOD STEW WITH EGGPLANT AND TOMATOES

SERVES 4 TO 6 AS AN APPETIZER

IL CLASSICO

Caponata is a spicy, tangy eggplant and tomato dish that originated in Sicily and features many of that town's most beloved ingredients, like anchovies and capers.

LA MIA VERSIONE

This recipe turns caponata into a vehicle for shellfish, which results in a happy marriage of earth and sea. Serve this with grilled croutons.

¾ CUP EXTRA VIRGIN OLIVE OIL

1 RED ONION, CUT INTO THIN WEDGES

1 LARGE CARROT, CUT INTO ¼-INCH DICE

1 CELERY RIB, CUT INTO ¼-INCH DICE

1 GREEN BELL PEPPER, CUT INTO ½-INCH DICE

1 YELLOW BELL PEPPER, CUT INTO ½-INCH DICE

1 EGGPLANT, TOP AND BOTTOM INCH CUT OFF, PEELED, SEEDED,
AND CUT INTO ½-INCH DICE

FINE SEA SALT

FRESHLY GROUND BLACK PEPPER

6 VINE-RIPENED TOMATOES, PEELED, SEEDED, AND CUT INTO ½-INCH DICE
(SEE NOTE, PAGE 25)

8 FRESH OREGANO LEAVES

4 GARLIC CLOVES, SLICED

2 PINCHES OF HOT RED PEPPER FLAKES

6 CUPS MUSSELS, BEARDED AND SCRUBBED

5 CUPS MANILA CLAMS, SCRUBBED AND RINSED

1 CUP DRY WHITE WINE

2 TABLESPOONS CHOPPED FRESH FLAT-LEAF PARSLEY

12 BAY SCALLOPS

GRILLED CROUTONS CUT FROM TUSCAN COUNTRY BREAD FOR GARNISH

(continued)

1 Warm 2 tablespoons of the olive oil in a wide deep sauté pan over medium heat. Add the onion, carrot, and celery and sauté until the onion is translucent, about 5 minutes. Remove the vegetables from the pan and set aside.

2 Warm 2 tablespoons of the remaining olive oil in the same pan and another 2 tablespoons in an additional sauté pan. Set both pans over medium-high heat. Add the green and yellow peppers to one, the eggplant to the other, and sauté for 5 minutes. Add the reserved onion, carrot, celery, and the peppers to the pan with the eggplant. Season with salt and pepper and stir well. Add the tomatoes and oregano and season with salt and pepper. Cook over medium-high heat until the vegetables are cooked but still firm, about 10 minutes. Transfer the vegetables to a bowl and set aside.

3 Warm 2 tablespoons of the remaining olive oil in each of the 2 sauté pans you used to cook the vegetables. Add half the garlic to each pan and sauté until golden, about 2 minutes. Add half the red pepper and the mussels to one pan and the rest of the red pepper and the clams to the other. Stir well, reduce the heat to low, and cover.

4 When the mussels and clams have opened, after about 3 minutes, pour half the wine into each pan. When the wine has evaporated, after about 2 minutes, sprinkle each pan with half the parsley and remove from the heat. Combine the contents of both pans in one.

5 Warm the remaining 2 tablespoons olive oil in a nonstick pan set over high heat. Add the scallops, season with salt and pepper, and cook until seared, about 1 minute per side.

6 Add the reserved vegetables to the pan with the mussels and clams, add the scallops, mix well, and cook for 5 minutes over low heat. Serve garnished with the croutons.

VINO The near-fizzy quality of Pinot Grigio suits this dish, especially if you can obtain one from the Trentino region.

PRESERVED TUNA AND OLIVE SALAD

———

SERVES 4 TO 6 AS AN APPETIZER

IL CLASSICO

In the United States, canned tuna is nothing special, something that's made into tuna salad sandwiches or simple casseroles, but in Italy preserved tuna, usually captured in a high-quality olive oil, is a treasured delicacy. The classic Tuscan preserved tuna salad features white cannellini beans and scallions.

LA MIA VERSIONE

This recipe shows you how to preserve your own tuna and then use it as the basis for a sophisticated salad. You need to prepare the tuna at least two days before you want to serve the salad, because the fish needs time to marinate.

JUICE OF 2 LEMONS

1¼ POUNDS TUNA LOIN

1½ CUPS DRY WHITE WINE

1 ONION WITH A CLOVE STUCK THROUGH ITS CENTER

1 SMALL CARROT

1 SMALL PIECE CELERY

1 LEEK, WHITE PART ONLY

2 TABLESPOONS COARSE SEA SALT

2 BAY LEAVES

2 TEASPOONS CORIANDER SEEDS

¼ JALAPEÑO PEPPER

2 FRESH THYME SPRIGS

1¾ CUPS PLUS 2 TABLESPOONS EXTRA VIRGIN OLIVE OIL

2 TABLESPOONS RED WINE VINEGAR

1 TEASPOON FINE SEA SALT

4 YUKON GOLD POTATOES, BOILED IN SALTED WATER, COOLED, AND CUT INTO ¾-INCH DICE

8 SCALLIONS, BOTH WHITE AND GREEN PARTS, SLICED ON THE BIAS

⅓ CUP NIÇOISE OLIVES

3 VINE-RIPENED TOMATOES, CUT INTO 8 WEDGES EACH

12 FRESH BASIL LEAVES

1 Fill a large bowl with 11 cups cold water and add the lemon juice. Place the tuna in the bowl, cover, and refrigerate for about 2 hours.

2 Fill a large bowl with ice water.

3 Make a court bouillon by pouring 5 cups of the tuna soaking water into a pot, then adding the wine, onion, carrot, celery, leek, and coarse salt. Bring the liquid to a boil over high heat, then reduce the heat and simmer for 20 minutes.

4 Drain the tuna and add it to the pot with the court bouillon. Cook for another 10 minutes. Set the pot in the ice water until the tuna has cooled, then remove the fish and drain it.

5 Break the tuna into 2- or 3-inch pieces and place them in a jar or terra-cotta bowl. Add the bay leaves, coriander seeds, jalapeño, and thyme and cover with 1½ cups of the oil. Store in the refrigerator. The tuna will taste best after a few days but will not last more than a week.

6 When ready to serve the salad, pour the vinegar into a salad bowl, add the fine sea salt, and whisk until the salt has dissolved. Add the remaining 6 tablespoons olive oil and whisk until the mixture has emulsified.

7 Place the potatoes in a mixing bowl and add the scallions, olives, tomatoes, basil leaves, and preserved tuna. Pour the oil-vinegar mixture on the salad and mix thoroughly. Divide among individual plates and serve.

VINO The olives in this dish make me long for Cannonau, a white wine from Sardinia, or any white Sicilian wine.

CHILEAN SEA BASS COOKED IN PARCHMENT PAPER WITH EGGPLANT AND TOMATOES

——

SERVES 4 AS A MAIN COURSE

IL CLASSICO

In cartoccio is the Italian phrase for a dish cooked in parchment paper; the method is traditionally used to prepare whole fish or shellfish.

LA MIA VERSIONE

This recipe applies a time-honored Italian cooking technique to a nonindigenous fish (Chilean sea bass), dividing it into four individual parchment packets, rather than one large one, allowing for a compelling presentation at the table.

3 EGGPLANTS, CUT INTO ¾-INCH DICE

FINE SEA SALT

3 CUPS CHERRY TOMATOES, HALVED

½ TEASPOON SUGAR

10 FRESH BASIL LEAVES, TORN BY HAND

1 FRESH ROSEMARY SPRIG

4 FRESH THYME SPRIGS

16 FRESH MINT LEAVES

2 TEASPOONS DRIED OREGANO

⅓ CUP EXTRA VIRGIN OLIVE OIL

1½ POUNDS CHILEAN SEA BASS FILLET, CUT INTO 4 PORTIONS

FRESHLY GROUND BLACK PEPPER

12 FRESH OREGANO LEAVES

¼ CUP DRY WHITE WINE

1 Preheat the oven to 250°F.

2 Place the diced eggplant in a colander, sprinkle with salt, and toss well. Let sit for 30 minutes to allow the salt to draw out the bitterness.

3 Line 2 sheet pans with parchment paper and arrange the tomatoes, cut side up, on one of them. Place 2 teaspoons salt in a small bowl, add the sugar, and stir. Sprinkle the mixture over the tomatoes. Add the basil leaves, rosemary, and thyme and bake until dry but not shriveled, about 40 minutes. Set aside.

4 Remove the eggplant from the colander and pat dry with a clean towel or paper towel. Place on another cookie sheet and bake until soft, about 30 minutes. Remove from the oven and raise the oven temperature to 400°F.

5 Transfer the cooked eggplant to a mixing bowl and add the mint leaves, dried oregano, and half the olive oil. Toss well.

6 Place each portion of fish on a piece of parchment paper about 11 x 13 inches. Season with salt and pepper. Arrange the eggplant, cherry tomatoes, and fresh oregano around the fish and drizzle the wine and remaining olive oil over the fish. Fold the

paper over, crimping it along the sides to form a sealed packet. Place the packets on a cookie sheet and bake for about 20 minutes.

7 Place one packet on each of 4 dinner plates. Cut them open and serve at once.

VINO A light young Riesling from the Veneto region will essentially act as a white wine sauce for this subtle dish.

BAKED SEA BREAM ON A BED OF POTATOES AND PECORINO

———

SERVES 4 AS A MAIN COURSE

IL CLASSICO

Orata al forno is a classic presentation in which fish is roasted atop a bed of potatoes.

LA MIA VERSIONE

It's very unorthodox to add cheese to any Italian seafood recipe, but the addition of Pecorino here infuses the entire fish with salty flavor.

3 CUPS CHERRY TOMATOES, HALVED

2 TEASPOONS FINE SEA SALT, PLUS MORE FOR SEASONING

½ TEASPOON SUGAR

10 FRESH BASIL LEAVES, TORN BY HAND

1 FRESH ROSEMARY SPRIG

4 FRESH THYME SPRIGS

⅓ CUP DRY WHITE WINE

⅓ CUP EXTRA VIRGIN OLIVE OIL

4 IDAHO POTATOES, SLICED CROSSWISE INTO ⅛-INCH-THICK SLICES AND BLANCHED

SIXTEEN ⅛-INCH-THICK SLICES PECORINO TOSCANO

⅓ CUP DRIED BREAD CRUMBS

GRATED ZEST OF ½ LEMON

SCANT PINCH OF CAYENNE PEPPER

1 TEASPOON DRIED OREGANO

FOUR 1-POUND SEA BREAM, FILLETED (8 FILLETS)

FRESHLY GROUND BLACK PEPPER

12 FRESH OREGANO LEAVES

2 TABLESPOONS GRATED PECORINO ROMANO

(continued)

1 Preheat the oven to 250°F.

2 Line a rimmed cookie sheet with parchment paper and arrange the tomatoes, cut side up, on it. Place the 2 teaspoons salt in a small bowl, add the sugar, and stir. Sprinkle the mixture over the tomatoes. Add the basil leaves, rosemary, and thyme and bake until dry but not shriveled, about 40 minutes. Remove from the oven and set aside. Raise the oven temperature to 400°F.

3 Coat 4 ovenproof terra-cotta or ceramic baking dishes (see Note), each wide and deep enough to hold one fish, with the wine and half the olive oil. Arrange the potato slices in them so they overlap. Place the tomatoes and sliced Pecorino Romano on top.

4 In a bowl, stir together the bread crumbs, lemon zest, cayenne pepper, and dried oregano.

5 Season the inside of the sea bream fillets with salt, black pepper, and fresh oregano. Place each half-fish on top of the other so the skin is facing outward, then place the fish on top of the potatoes and sprinkle both with the seasoned bread crumbs. Drizzle with the rest of the olive oil, sprinkle with the grated Pecorino Romano, cover with aluminum foil, and bake for 15 minutes.

6 Remove the foil and cook for about 10 more minutes, until the cheese on top is melted and the potatoes and fish are crispy. Serve each portion in its baking dish.

VINO A young, fruity Vermentino from Cinque Terre, Liguria, will cut through the richness of the bream.

NOTE: The individual baking dishes make a beautiful presentation, but if you don't have any, cook the entire dish in one large roasting pan, arranging the layers of potatoes, tomatoes, and cheese as indicated in the recipe, and top with the fillets in a single layer.

HALIBUT STEAMED WITH LEMON LEAVES AND ASPARAGUS

——————

SERVES 4 AS A MAIN COURSE

IL CLASSICO

This recipe may remind you of the Italian tradition of serving grilled fish with a wedge of lemon and olive oil.

LA MIA VERSIONE

Marta Pulini was inspired to create this dish by the Asian cuisine she discovered in New York City.

1½ POUNDS HALIBUT FILLET, CUT INTO 4 PIECES

FINE SEA SALT

FRESHLY GROUND BLACK PEPPER

6 SCALLIONS, BOTH WHITE AND GREEN PARTS, THINLY SLICED

JUICE OF 4 LEMONS

½ CUP PLUS 2 TABLESPOONS EXTRA VIRGIN OLIVE OIL

ENOUGH UNSPRAYED LEMON LEAVES (AVAILABLE FROM FARMERS' MARKETS AND FLORISTS) TO COVER THE BOTTOM OF A STEAMER BASKET

2 BUNCHES ASPARAGUS, PEELED, THE TOUGH PART OF THE STEMS REMOVED

2 TABLESPOONS MINCED FRESH CHIVES

1 Place the halibut in a nonreactive baking pan large enough to hold the fish in a single layer and season with salt and pepper. Scatter and drizzle the scallions, lemon juice, and half the olive oil over the fish. Cover with plastic wrap and marinate in the refrigerator for 1 hour.

2 Set a shallow pot of water (sized to hold a steamer basket) to simmer over high heat.

3 Cover the bottom of a steamer basket with the lemon leaves. Remove the fish from the marinade and place in the basket. Steam, covered, over the simmering water for 20 to 25 minutes, until cooked through.

4 Fill a large bowl with ice water. Set aside.

5 Pour enough water into a pot to completely immerse the asparagus. Season lightly with salt and bring to a boil. Add the asparagus and cook for 3 to 4 minutes.

6 Remove the asparagus with tongs and plunge them in the ice water to stop the cooking and preserve their verdant color.

7 Divide the lemon leaves among 4 serving plates and top with the fish. Arrange the asparagus on the side, sprinkle with chives, and drizzle with the remaining olive oil.

VINO What do you serve with something this lemony? A sparkling Prosecco from the Veneto, with hints of vanilla.

TONNO ALLE OLIVE E VINO ROSSO

GRILLED TUNA WITH OLIVES AND RED WINE

———

SERVES 4 AS A MAIN COURSE

IL CLASSICO

Grilled tuna is an American staple, usually served with a simple green salad or grilled vegetables like potatoes and corn.

LA MIA VERSIONE

This recipe takes grilled tuna to new heights with a pan sauce of olives, fennel, and red wine.

⅓ CUP EXTRA VIRGIN OLIVE OIL

4 RED ONIONS, SLICED INTO ⅛-INCH-THICK RINGS

2 FENNEL BULBS, SLICED HORIZONTALLY ⅛ INCH THICK, FRONDS RESERVED

FINE SEA SALT

FRESHLY GROUND BLACK PEPPER

½ CUP YOUNG CHIANTI

8 VINE-RIPENED TOMATOES, PEELED, SEEDED, AND ROUGHLY CHOPPED (SEE NOTE, PAGE 25)

⅓ CUP GREEN KALAMATA OLIVES, PITTED

⅓ CUP BLACK GAETA OLIVES, PITTED

FOUR ½-POUND TUNA STEAKS

1 Warm half the olive oil in a sauté pan over medium heat. Add the onions and fennel and sauté until the fennel has almost caramelized, about 25 minutes.

2 Season to taste with salt and pepper, increase the heat to high, and add the wine. Let the alcohol evaporate, about 1 minute, then add the tomatoes, stirring well. Season to taste with salt and pepper and add the fennel fronds and green and black olives. Cook for about 15 more minutes, until the sauce has reached a creamy consistency.

3 Prepare an outdoor grill and cook the tuna steaks to the desired doneness.

4 Spoon some sauce on each of 4 dinner plates and serve the tuna steaks on top of the sauce. Drizzle with the remaining olive oil.

VINO For this Sicilian-inspired dish, go with a good dry Sicilian white wine: Regaleali.

RED SNAPPER WITH A CLAM AND FAVA BEAN SAUCE

———

SERVES 4 AS A MAIN COURSE

IL CLASSICO

Guazzetto is a method of cooking seafood in a light sauce of white wine, garlic, parsley, and tomato. This delicate treatment preserves the character of the fish, complementing it with just enough aromatic flavor. (*Guazzetto* can also refer to meat dishes cooked in a similar mixture, with stock instead of wine.)

LA MIA VERSIONE

It occurred to me that this technique is similar to the most common way of cooking clams. So, in this recipe, we create complexity by preparing clams, then using their flavorful liquid as a cooking medium for the fish. Dentice (a Mediterranean fish named for its sharp teeth) would be my choice in Tuscany, but it's unavailable in the United States. I've substituted a very similar fish: red snapper. To underscore the fresh flavors, we add fava beans at the end. Don't bother to blanch them; they'll cook just enough in the hot *jus*.

---

1 CUP VEGETABLE STOCK

½ CUP EXTRA VIRGIN OLIVE OIL

3 GARLIC CLOVES, CRUSHED AND PEELED

3 PINCHES OF HOT RED PEPPER FLAKES

60 MANILA CLAMS, SCRUBBED AND RINSED

20 CHERRY TOMATOES, HALVED

½ CUP DRY WHITE WINE

FINE SEA SALT

FOUR 7-OUNCE RED SNAPPER FILLETS

FRESHLY GROUND BLACK PEPPER

1 CUP SHELLED FRESH FAVA BEANS, PEELED (BLANCHED FIRST FOR EASIER PEELING IF DESIRED), FROM ABOUT 2 POUNDS IN THE POD (SEE NOTE, PAGE 80)

1 TABLESPOON MINCED FRESH FLAT-LEAF PARSLEY

1 Preheat the oven to 450°F.

2 Pour the vegetable stock into a small pot and bring it to a simmer.

3 Heat the olive oil in an ovenproof sauté pan deep and wide enough to hold the fish in one layer. Add the garlic, red pepper, and clams, cover with a lid or an inverted pan of the same size, and cook until the clams have opened, about 5 minutes.

4 Add the tomatoes and cook until wilted, about 30 seconds. Add the wine and cook until the wine evaporates, about 2 minutes. Season with salt.

5 Remove three-quarters of the clams from the pan. Set aside.

6 Add the hot stock to the pan with the remaining clams, raise the heat, and bring it to a boil. Add the snapper to the pan, season with salt and black pepper, cover with aluminum foil, and transfer to the preheated oven. Bake for 15 minutes.

(continued)

7 While the fish is cooking, remove the reserved clams from their shells.

8 Remove the pan from the oven. Scatter the reserved clams, fava beans, and parsley over the pan. Taste and adjust the seasoning if necessary. Divide the fish among individual bowls, spooning some clams and *jus* over each serving.

VINO Serve this springtime dish with a light, crisp Sauvignon Blanc from New Zealand, well chilled.

BRAISED SALMON FILLET WITH SAVOY CABBAGE AND BLACK TRUFFLE

———

SERVES 4 AS A MAIN COURSE

IL CLASSICO

While black cabbage and pancetta are a popular combination, green cabbage is usually used in fish dishes or vegetable soups, because it has a less assertive flavor.

LA MIA VERSIONE

Salmon has enough fatty richness to stand up to the strong flavors of cabbage and bacon, used here as a cooking medium for the fish itself.

FINE SEA SALT

6 CUPS TIGHTLY PACKED SAVOY CABBAGE LEAVES, RINSED AND SLICED ½ INCH THICK

¼ CUP PLUS 2 TABLESPOONS EXTRA VIRGIN OLIVE OIL

1 ONION, CHOPPED

1 CUP FINELY DICED BACON

1 OUNCE BLACK TRUFFLE

1½ POUNDS SKINLESS SALMON FILLET, CUT INTO 4 PORTIONS

FRESHLY GROUND BLACK PEPPER

1 Preheat the oven to 400°F.

2 Pour enough water into a stockpot to completely immerse the cabbage. Add salt and bring the liquid to a boil. Add the cabbage leaves and blanch them for 3 to 4 minutes, then drain them, reserving 1 cup of the cooking water.

3 Warm ¼ cup of the olive oil in a sauté pan over medium heat. Add the onion and bacon and sauté until brown, about 4 minutes. Reduce the heat to low, add the cabbage and the cooking liquid, and sauté for about 30 minutes, until the cabbage is tender and juicy.

4 Divide the cabbage into 4 portions and place each in a terra-cotta or ceramic ovenproof baking pan (see Note). Shave the truffle over the portions. Season the salmon with salt, pepper, and the rest of the olive oil, then place it on top of the cabbage. Cover with aluminum foil and bake for 10 minutes. Remove the foil and bake for about 10 more minutes, depending on how well cooked you desire the salmon. Serve in the individual baking dishes.

VINO This dish is very complex in taste, so pair it with the most complex and elegant Italian red wine, Barbaresco.

NOTE: You can cook this dish in one large roasting pan, arranging the cabbage as indicated in the recipe, and top with the fillets in a single layer.

SEAFOOD STEW WITH ITS OWN BREAD CRUST

SERVES 4 AS A MAIN COURSE

IL CLASSICO

This recipe is inspired by cioppino, the Italian-American answer to cacciucco, described on page 7.

LA MIA VERSIONE

This recipe returns to the rustic origins of the original cacciucco, baking a bread crust over each individual crock. Although scorfano, or scorpion fish, is the basis of a cacciucco (and bouillabaisse), it is virtually impossible to find here. You can substitute Chilean sea bass or any rockfish.

You will need four crocks, about 5 inches wide and 3 inches deep (the shape is not important).

BREAD CRUST

4 CUPS DURUM FLOUR (SEE IN SEARCH OF . . . , PAGE 16) OR ALL-PURPOSE FLOUR, PLUS MORE FOR DUSTING THE WORK SURFACE

¾ OUNCE FRESH YEAST

2 TEASPOONS FINE SEA SALT

2 PINCHES OF SAFFRON THREADS

¼ CUP EXTRA VIRGIN OLIVE OIL

1 Dust a work surface with flour and mound the 4 cups flour on it. Make a well in the center.

2 Dissolve the yeast in a bowl with ¾ cup warm water.

3 Place the salt, yeast, saffron, and olive oil in the well and, with the help of a fork, incorporate the flour into them. Add more water as needed to make a homogenous, elastic dough.

4 Dust a bowl roughly double the size of the dough with flour and place the dough in the bowl. Cover with plastic wrap and set it in a warm place to proof for about 2 hours; when the dough is proofed (the volume will be doubled), knead it on a flour-dusted surface until very smooth, then divide it into 4 parts and roll them, one at a time, with a rolling pin to make a circle about 7 inches in diameter.

FISH STOCK

1 Place all the ingredients in a pot, cover by 1 inch with cold water, and bring to a boil over high heat. Lower the heat and simmer for about 40 minutes, skimming any foam and impurities that rise to the surface.

2 Strain the stock through a fine-mesh strainer set over a bowl. Discard the solids.

1½ POUNDS FRESH FISH SKELETONS FROM NONOILY WHITE FISH SUCH AS HALIBUT OR COD, WASHED

1 ONION, ROUGHLY CHOPPED

1 CARROT, ROUGHLY CHOPPED

1 CELERY RIB, ROUGHLY CHOPPED

¼ CUP EXTRA VIRGIN OLIVE OIL

1 HERB SACHET: 3 FRESH THYME SPRIGS, 1 BAY LEAF, 10 FRESH FLAT-LEAF PARSLEY SPRIGS, AND 5 CELERY LEAVES, TIED WITH KITCHEN STRING

CIOPPINO

1 Warm the olive oil over low heat in a flameproof casserole large enough to hold the fish. Add the onion and sauté until translucent, about 15 minutes. Add the garlic, the parsley, the red pepper, and the saffron. Add the fish and brown it on all sides, seasoning with salt and black pepper as you turn it. Add the wine and let it evaporate, 3 to 4 minutes; then add the tomatoes, taste, and adjust the seasoning with salt and black pepper. Cook over low heat for 15 minutes, then add the hot fish stock and cook for 30 more minutes, until the fish falls apart.

2 Preheat the oven to 350°F.

3 Pass the contents of the pot, bones and all, through a food mill to get as much flavor as possible from the fish (remove the head if it does not fit). Transfer the sauce to a sauté pan, bring to a boil over high heat, taste, and adjust the seasoning.

4 Divide the sauce among the 4 crocks. Season the monkfish, scallops, shrimp, and mussels with salt and black pepper and divide them equally among the crocks. Brush the edges of the crocks with water and place the bread dough on top of each. Bake for about 25 minutes, until the bread dough is golden and crusty. Serve in the individual crocks.

VINO Serve this with a young Vernaccia, a crisp white wine from Tuscany.

⅓ CUP EXTRA VIRGIN OLIVE OIL

1 ONION, CHOPPED

2 GARLIC CLOVES, CHOPPED

2 TABLESPOONS CHOPPED FRESH FLAT-LEAF PARSLEY

¼ TEASPOON HOT RED PEPPER FLAKES

2 PINCHES OF SAFFRON THREADS

THREE 1-POUND SCORFANO (SCORPION FISH) OR 3 POUNDS ROCKFISH OR CHILEAN SEA BASS, GUTTED AND SCALED

FINE SEA SALT

FRESHLY GROUND BLACK PEPPER

1 CUP CHIANTI

ONE 16-OUNCE CAN TOMATOES

2 CUPS FISH STOCK

¾ POUND MONKFISH TAIL, CUT INTO 1½-INCH PIECES

12 SEA SCALLOPS

12 SHRIMP, SHELLED AND DEVEINED

16 MUSSELS, BEARDED AND SCRUBBED

PAN-SEARED SOFT-SHELL CRABS WITH LEMON, CAPERS, AND OLIVES

——

SERVES 4 AS A MAIN COURSE

IL CLASSICO

Lemons, capers, and olives are traditional accompaniments to seafood throughout Italy and, indeed, all over the Mediterranean.

LA MIA VERSIONE

Here we apply the simple Tuscan sensibility to soft-shell crabs, which, incidentally, are not available in Italy.

---

1 CUP SEMOLINA FLOUR

½ CUP ALL-PURPOSE FLOUR

12 SOFT-SHELL CRABS, WITH THE APRONS REMOVED BY THE FISHMONGER

¼ CUP PLUS 2 TABLESPOONS EXTRA VIRGIN OLIVE OIL

3 TABLESPOONS UNSALTED BUTTER

FINE SEA SALT

FRESHLY GROUND BLACK PEPPER

⅓ CUP DRY WHITE WINE

JUICE OF 3 LEMONS

⅓ CUP DRAINED CAPERS

1 TABLESPOON CHOPPED FRESH FLAT-LEAF PARSLEY

4 CUPS TIGHTLY PACKED ARUGULA, STEMS REMOVED, RINSED, AND SPUN DRY

1 BUNCH WATERCRESS, STEMS REMOVED, RINSED, AND SPUN DRY

3 LEMONS, ZEST AND PITH REMOVED, CUT INTO WEDGES

16 CAPER BERRIES

1 Sift the semolina flour and all-purpose flour together and dust the crabs with it.

2 Warm 2 tablespoons of the olive oil in a sauté pan large enough to hold the crabs in one layer over medium heat, then add 2 tablespoons of the butter. When the butter has melted, add the crabs and sauté on both sides, seasoning with salt and pepper, until crispy, 2 to 3 minutes per side. Remove the crabs and keep them warm.

3 Add the wine to the sauté pan. When it has evaporated, add two-thirds of the lemon juice, the capers, the rest of the butter, and the chopped parsley. Cook for 1 to 2 minutes more, until the sauce is creamy.

4 Pour the remaining lemon juice into a mixing bowl, add ¼ teaspoon salt, and whisk until the salt has dissolved. Add the remaining ¼ cup olive oil and whisk until well mixed.

5 Place the arugula in a salad bowl and add the watercress, lemon wedges, and caper berries. Add the lemon-juice-and-oil mixture and mix well.

6 Serve the crabs with the sauce on top and the salad on the side.

VINO A South African Chardonnay will play beautifully off the crabmeat and the peppery arugula.

SPAGHETTI CON GRANSEOLA AL POMODORO PICCANTE

DUNGENESS CRAB PASTA WITH ROASTED TOMATO AND BELL PEPPER SAUCE

——

SERVES 6 AS AN APPETIZER OR 4 AS A MAIN COURSE

IL CLASSICO

Pasta arrabbiata (angry pasta) is a hot and spicy Italian classic made with lots of garlic and hot red pepper flakes.

LA MIA VERSIONE

This recipe adds one of the greatest North American shellfish, Dungeness crab, to the formula for one of Italy's greatest pasta sauces.

---

2 DUNGENESS CRABS

24 CHERRY TOMATOES, HALVED

1½ TEASPOONS FINE SEA SALT MIXED WITH 1½ TEASPOONS SUGAR

12 FRESH BASIL LEAVES

2 FRESH ROSEMARY SPRIGS

6 FRESH THYME SPRIGS

1 RED BELL PEPPER

1 YELLOW BELL PEPPER

⅓ CUP EXTRA VIRGIN OLIVE OIL

⅓ CUP CHOPPED RED ONION

2 GARLIC CLOVES, CHOPPED

½ CUP DRY WHITE WINE

PINCH OF HOT RED PEPPER FLAKES

¾ POUND SPAGHETTI

1 TABLESPOON CHOPPED FRESH FLAT-LEAF PARSLEY

1 Preheat the oven to 200°F.

2 Blanch the crabs in boiling water for 5 minutes, then drain them and let them cool to room temperature. Once they have cooled, open them and remove all the meat from the body and claws. Reserve the shells and claws. Roughly chop the meat and set it aside separately.

3 Line a rimmed cookie sheet with parchment paper and place the cherry tomatoes, cut side up, on it. Sprinkle with the salt-sugar mixture, then scatter the basil, rosemary, and thyme over the tomatoes. Bake until dry but not shriveled, 45 to 60 minutes, then remove from the oven and set aside until the tomatoes cool to room temperature.

4 Roast the bell peppers over the flame of a gas burner, turning them frequently with the help of a long fork or tongs to roast them evenly on all sides. Place them in a bowl sealed with plastic wrap for half an hour, then peel them, removing all the burned skin; to make this easier, you can peel the peppers under running water. Cut the peppers into 1-inch-wide strips.

5 Heat half the olive oil in a sauté pan over medium heat. Add the onion and garlic and sauté until translucent, about 4 minutes. Add the wine, let it evaporate, about 2 minutes, then add the tomatoes and bell peppers. Simmer for about 10 minutes,

adding a cup of water if the sauce gets too dry, then turn the contents of the pan out into the bowl of a food processor and puree it.

6 Return the sauce to the sauté pan and stir the crabmeat into it. Simmer over low heat. Add the red pepper and cook for 2 more minutes.

7 Bring a pot of salted water to a boil and cook the spaghetti until al dente, about 9 minutes, depending on the brand. Reserve about 1 cup cooking liquid, then drain the spaghetti. Stir the spaghetti into the sauce and mix well, adding a few tablespoons of cooking liquid if the sauce becomes too dry. Sprinkle with parsley and drizzle with the rest of the olive oil.

IN SEARCH OF . . . DUNGENESS CRAB
Dungeness crabs flourish from Alaska to central California and are especially plentiful in the waters near Washington State. They can grow as big as 3 pounds.

VINO A full-bodied California Chardonnay will cool off your palate as you eat this spicy pasta.

FETTUCCINE WITH MUSHROOMS, SHRIMP, AND WHITE WINE

———

SERVES 6 AS AN APPETIZER OR 4 AS A PASTA

IL CLASSICO

Fettuccine e funghi, or fresh egg pasta with mushrooms, is a classic Italian dish that is so popular it is adapted for each season: served with fresh porcini in white sauce in the summer, with tomato sauce in the fall, and in the winter—when we are dying for the rich, earthy flavor of porcini—with a sauce of dried porcini and tomato.

LA MIA VERSIONE

This recipe adds shrimp, which have a mouthfeel that complements the porcini.

DOUGH

3½ CUPS DURUM FLOUR (SEE IN SEARCH OF . . . , PAGE 16) OR ALL-PURPOSE FLOUR

4 LARGE EGGS

SEMOLINA FLOUR FOR DUSTING A LARGE TRAY

1 Place the flour on a clean work surface and make a well in the center; place the eggs in the middle and mix them into the flour a little at a time, with the help of a fork. Knead until the dough has a smooth and even consistency.

2 Roll the dough out with a lightly floured rolling pin or run it through a pasta machine to make sheets about ⅛ inch thick. Then pass the sheets through the fettuccine attachment or let the rolled dough dry slightly, dust it with flour, and roll it up loosely. Slice the roll into strips ⅜ inch wide. Spread the fettuccine over a large tray dusted with flour.

SAUCE AND ASSEMBLY

1 Heat one-third of the olive oil over medium heat in a skillet large enough to hold the mushrooms without crowding. Add half the garlic and sauté until golden brown, 1 or 2 minutes. Add the mushrooms and sauté them, seasoning with salt, black pepper, and half the thyme leaves, for 5 minutes. Remove from the heat and set aside.

2 Heat another third of the olive oil in a skillet over medium heat. Add the remaining garlic and the red pepper and cook until the garlic is browned, about 2 minutes. Add the shrimp, season with salt and black pepper, and when the shrimp are golden brown on both sides, after about 3 minutes, pour in the wine and let it evaporate, about 2 minutes. Cook for another 2 to 3 minutes, then turn the shrimp and their sauce into the skillet with the mushrooms.

3 Bring a pot of salted water to a boil and cook the fettuccine for 2 to 3 minutes after they float. Reserve ¼ cup of the cooking liquid, then strain the pasta in a colander. Transfer the pasta to a large bowl and add the mushrooms and shrimp. Toss well, adding the rest of the thyme leaves and the last third of the olive oil. If it seems too dry, stir in some of the reserved pasta cooking liquid.

VINO The uncommon combination of porcini and shrimp calls for an uncommon wine: Cortese di Gavi, a gentle white from Piemonte.

⅓ CUP EXTRA VIRGIN OLIVE OIL

4 GARLIC CLOVES, SLICED

1½ POUNDS FRESH PORCINI OR OTHER FRESH MUSHROOMS, SUCH AS OYSTERS AND SHIITAKE, SAND REMOVED WITH A DAMP TOWEL AND SLICED, BOTH CAP AND STEM, ¼ INCH THICK

FINE SEA SALT

FRESHLY GROUND BLACK PEPPER

2 TABLESPOONS FRESH THYME LEAVES

PINCH OF HOT RED PEPPER FLAKES

24 MEDIUM SHRIMP, SHELLED AND DEVEINED

½ CUP DRY WHITE WINE

OPEN-FACE LOBSTER WITH TUSCAN BREADING

———

SERVES 4 AS A MAIN COURSE

IL CLASSICO

In Italy one of the most popular ways to cook lobster is stuffed with a mixture of its own tomalley, bread crumbs, salt, and pepper.

LA MIA VERSIONE

This recipe produces a more elegant lobster thanks largely to the use of Vin Santo as a basting element, but the bread crumbs are still present in the sauce. Serve this with Barley Risotto with Fava Beans and Pecorino Toscano (page 83).

FOUR 1½-POUND LOBSTERS

4 TABLESPOONS (½ STICK) UNSALTED BUTTER

PINCH OF FRESHLY GROUND WHITE PEPPER

PINCH OF FRESHLY GRATED NUTMEG

¼ TEASPOON CAYENNE PEPPER

⅓ CUP VIN SANTO

FINE SEA SALT

2 TABLESPOONS DRIED BREAD CRUMBS

1 Preheat the broiler.

2 Fill a pot with enough water to completely immerse the lobsters, then bring it to a boil. Add the lobsters and cook for 5 minutes, remove them from the pot with tongs, let them cool, and cut them in half lengthwise.

3 Place the butter in a small pan and add the white pepper, nutmeg, cayenne pepper, and Vin Santo and season with salt. Mix well and set over medium-high heat. When the wine has evaporated, remove the sauce from the heat. Stir in the bread crumbs.

4 Place the lobsters, cut side up, on a cookie sheet and brush them with the sauce. Cook them under the broiler for 10 to 15 minutes, basting them continuously with the sauce to keep them moist; if they get too brown, cover them with aluminum foil.

5 Remove from the oven, place on individual plates, and serve at once.

VINO Cortese di Gavi (Piemonte), one of the few great whites of Piemonte, is elegant enough to serve with lobster.

CALAMARI RIPIENI AL FARRO

CALAMARI STUFFED WITH LEMON ZEST, SPELT, AND ONIONS

———

SERVES 4 AS A MAIN COURSE

IL CLASSICO

Calamari are most often used in Tuscan cooking, where they are sliced into rings and deep-fried, stewed in a sauce of tomato and peas, or stuffed with bread.

LA MIA VERSIONE

Spelt makes a substantial stuffing for calamari. Use only a few teaspoons of filling per squid, because they will shrink as they cook.

1 Preheat the oven to 300°F.

2 Warm a quarter of the olive oil in a sauté pan over medium-high heat. Add the onion and half the garlic and sauté for 2 to 3 minutes. Add the tentacles, season with salt and pepper, and cook for 10 minutes. Stir in half the wine and cook until it evaporates, about 4 minutes. Remove from the heat.

3 Bring a pot of lightly salted water to a boil over high heat. Add the spelt and cook for about 15 minutes, then drain it and place it in a bowl.

4 Roughly chop the anchovies, capers, and remaining garlic together and stir into the spelt. Add the lemon zest, 1 tablespoon of the parsley, and ¼ cup of the remaining olive oil. Stuff the calamari with this mixture and seal them with a toothpick.

5 Heat the rest of the olive oil in an ovenproof sauté pan. Add the calamari and sauté until lightly browned on all sides. Add the cherry tomatoes, season with salt and pepper, being mindful that the anchovy and caper stuffing is salty, then sprinkle with the remaining wine. When the wine has evaporated, about 4 minutes, add the stock, cover the pan with aluminum foil, and bake for 20 minutes. Remove the foil and cook for 10 more minutes. Remove the toothpicks and top with sauce and parsley.

VINO Pick something that will underscore the seaside spirit of this dish, like a good Montepulciano d'Abruzzo.

¾ CUP EXTRA VIRGIN OLIVE OIL

⅓ CUP CHOPPED RED ONION

4 GARLIC CLOVES, MINCED

12 MEDIUM CALAMARI, CLEANED AND RINSED, TENTACLES SET ASIDE

FINE SEA SALT

FRESHLY GROUND BLACK PEPPER

1½ CUPS DRY WHITE WINE

½ CUP PLUS 2 TABLESPOONS SPELT, SOAKED IN COLD WATER FOR 2 HOURS AND DRAINED

8 ANCHOVY FILLETS IN OLIVE OIL

¼ CUP DRAINED CAPERS

GRATED ZEST OF 1 LEMON

2 TABLESPOONS CHOPPED FRESH FLAT-LEAF PARSLEY

16 CHERRY TOMATOES, HALVED

½ CUP VEGETABLE STOCK

POLLAME
POULTRY

When I first learned that the national symbol of the United States was the bald eagle, I was surprised. Because I thought that if the symbol of the United States was a bird, it could have been the chicken. Not because I think Americans are chicken, but because Americans *eat* more chicken than anyone else in the world. They eat it fried. They eat it grilled. They eat it roasted. They eat it barbecued. They eat it in four-star restaurants, and they eat it in fast-food chains.

But my adopted cocitizens confuse me. They seem to love chicken, so much so that many of them eat it three or four times a week. What's incredible is that they don't do very much with it. It usually just gets marinated, then tossed into the pan or the oven, often without the skin, which is a great source of flavor. It seems like nothing but a convenient source of protein that's easy to handle, especially when purchased in prebutchered sections ready to be cooked.

In Tuscany, chicken is served no more or less than rabbit, duck, and game. My mother, for example, would have been able to make cacciatore with rabbit or game just as easily as with chicken. But she knew how to make the chicken itself taste great, or rather, she *let* it taste great. One of the reasons she was so talented with chicken is that she saw it butchered in person, brought it home fresh, and knew enough to give it just a short time in the pan. Even when it was surrounded by the ingredients of a ragout, cacciatore, or stew, she never let the bird itself overcook. So its flavor stood out more than any other ingredient in the dish, unlike the chicken in a lot of American kitchens, which seems to be used like tofu—as a neutral ingredient to soak up the other flavors.

A people who believe in using *every* part of an animal, Tuscans are adept not just with chicken meat but also with chicken liver. If you only know this delicacy as the "Jewish foie gras," then you haven't tried such dishes as Chicken Consommé with Chicken Liver and Square Pasta or Chicken Liver Fricassee. Try them now. Trust me: you'll never think of chicken liver the same way again.

Along the same lines, do yourself a favor and try the Cornish hen and baby chicken recipes in this chapter: they allow you to savor the benefits of cooking with a *whole* animal—great flavor and *no* waste—without having to butcher it.

One final word of advice: seek out the best chicken you can find, preferably organic. That way, even if you do something as simple as just throwing it under the broiler, it'll taste like something worthwhile.

CHICKEN SALAD WITH HAM, GRUYÈRE, AND VEGETABLES

SERVES 6 AS AN APPETIZER

IL CLASSICO

A simple salad of diced poached chicken, mayonnaise, and vegetables is an American staple.

LA MIA VERSIONE

This recipe, based on one made by Marta's grandmother (Marta Pulini is my corporate chef and recipe collaborator in this book), takes the chicken salad to new heights. It resembles the American dish but has a complex flavor thanks to salty ham, sharp Gruyère cheese, and the full flavor of extra virgin olive oil.

1 ONION

1 CARROT

1 CELERY RIB

FINE SEA SALT

1 WHOLE CHICKEN BREAST, BONED, RINSED, AND PATTED DRY

JUICE OF 1 LEMON

¼ CUP EXTRA VIRGIN OLIVE OIL

ONE 7-OUNCE SLICE BOILED HAM, JULIENNED INTO STRIPS 1 INCH LONG AND ⅛ INCH WIDE

ONE 7-OUNCE SLICE GRUYÈRE, JULIENNED INTO STRIPS 1 INCH LONG AND ⅛ INCH WIDE

1 CUP FRESH CORN KERNELS

½ CUP MAYONNAISE

1 ROMAINE LETTUCE HEART, SLICED INTO ¼-INCH-WIDE STRIPS

FRESHLY GROUND BLACK PEPPER

BIBB LETTUCE LEAVES, RINSED AND SPUN DRY, FOR GARNISH

1 Place the onion, carrot, and celery in a pot. Cover with cold water and lightly salt the water. Bring to a boil over high heat. Lower the heat and let simmer for about ½ hour, then add the chicken breast and cook for about 25 minutes or until a sharp, thin-bladed knife inserted to the center reveals no red and only a hint of pink, if any. Use tongs to remove the breast from the stock and let it cool. (Strain and reserve the broth for another use.) When the breast is cold, dice it into ½-inch squares.

2 In a mixing bowl, dissolve ½ teaspoon salt in the lemon juice. Stirring with a whisk, add the olive oil in a thin stream.

3 In a large bowl, toss together the chicken, ham, Gruyère, corn kernels, mayonnaise, and lemon vinaigrette. At the end, stir in the romaine lettuce, mixing continuously. Taste and season with black pepper and additional salt if necessary.

4 Arrange the Bibb lettuce leaves all around the serving bowl and place the chicken salad in it. Serve, if you like, with toasted bread.

VINO Enjoy this cold lunchtime salad with a dry, well-chilled sparkling Prosecco from the Veneto region.

CHICKEN CONSOMMÉ WITH CHICKEN LIVER AND SQUARE PASTA

———

SERVES 6 AS A SOUP

IL CLASSICO

"Little squares" of pasta known as *quadrucci* are usually stuffed and added to soups. They are especially beloved as a vehicle for adding sautéed chicken livers to beef stock.

LA MIA VERSIONE

In this recipe we intensify the stock itself with the addition of chicken liver and add the pasta as a separate element, making it unnecessary to go to the trouble of stuffing the quadrucci.

CHICKEN BROTH

1 MEDIUM CHICKEN, RINSED AND PATTED DRY

1 ONION

1 CARROT

1 CELERY RIB

COARSE SALT

Place the chicken, onion, carrot, and celery in a large pot and season lightly with salt. Add water to cover, bring to a boil over high heat, then lower the heat and simmer for about 1 hour, frequently skimming any foam or impurities that rise to the surface. Pass the broth through a very-fine-mesh strainer and reserve.

CHICKEN LIVERS

4 CHICKEN LIVERS, TRIMMED AND RINSED

¼ CUP BRANDY

1 TABLESPOON UNSALTED BUTTER

1½ TEASPOONS CHOPPED SHALLOT

2 FRESH SAGE LEAVES

FINE SEA SALT

FRESHLY GROUND BLACK PEPPER

1 Soak the chicken livers in the brandy for 2 to 3 hours, then strain over a bowl, reserving the livers and brandy separately.

2 Melt the butter in a sauté pan over medium-high heat. Add the shallot and sauté until translucent, about 2 minutes. Add the chicken livers and sage and season with salt and pepper. Sauté for 5 minutes, then add the reserved brandy and let the alcohol evaporate, about 2 minutes; remove from the heat and let cool to warm. Turn the chicken livers out onto a cutting board and roughly chop them. Set aside.

(continued)

½ CUP DURUM FLOUR (SEE IN SEARCH OF . . . ,
PAGE 16) OR ALL-PURPOSE FLOUR

1 LARGE EGG

SEMOLINA FLOUR FOR DUSTING PANS

FINE SEA SALT

FRESHLY GROUND BLACK PEPPER

GRATED PARMIGIANO-REGGIANO (OPTIONAL)

PASTA

Place the flour on a smooth, clean surface and make a well in the middle. Place the egg in the well and mix it into the flour a little at a time with the help of a fork; then knead until the dough has a smooth and even consistency. Roll the dough through a pasta machine to make thin sheets about ⅛ inch thick. Roll the pasta sheets and cut them horizontally into ¼-inch strips and then crosswise to obtain ¼-inch squares; spread them out on a sheet pan dusted with semolina flour.

SOUP AND ASSEMBLY

1 Pour the chicken broth into a pot and bring to a boil over high heat. Taste and adjust the seasoning if necessary. Add the pasta. Cook for 2 to 3 minutes.

2 Meanwhile, spoon 1 tablespoon of the chicken livers into each of 4 large bowls.

3 Ladle some soup into each bowl and sprinkle with grated Parmigiano if you like. Serve at once.

VINO The rich chicken livers demand something earthy, like a young Rosso di Montalcino from Tuscany.

FRICASSEA DI FEGATINI DI POLLO

CHICKEN LIVER FRICASSEE

———————

SERVES 4 AS AN APPETIZER

IL CLASSICO

This recipe takes its inspiration from chicken liver Fiorentina, traditionally prepared with brown butter and sage.

LA MIA VERSIONE

Here we've added egg yolk and lemon juice to give the dish a more velvety texture and to enliven it with extra acidity.

1 Melt the butter with the olive oil in a skillet over medium heat. Add the onion and bay leaves and cook until the onion is translucent, about 5 minutes. Stir in the chicken livers and sage and brown them on all sides, seasoning with salt and pepper.

2 Add the wine and reduce until dry, 1 to 2 minutes.

3 Meanwhile, place the egg yolks in a small bowl and thin them with the lemon juice.

4 Remove the pan from the heat and immediately add the egg-lemon mixture, stirring vigorously to blend in the eggs and create a very creamy sauce. (Be sure to do this off the heat or the eggs will curdle.) Stir in the parsley.

VINO Serve this with a sparkling light red Barbera from Emilia-Romagna if you can find it. (I actually recommend this wine slightly chilled.) You can also use Vino Novello, the Italian equivalent of Beaujolais Nouveau, or any light-bodied red wine.

1 TABLESPOON UNSALTED BUTTER

2 TABLESPOONS EXTRA VIRGIN OLIVE OIL

1 TABLESPOON CHOPPED ONION

2 BAY LEAVES

3 CUPS CHICKEN LIVERS, TRIMMED, MEMBRANES REMOVED, AND RINSED

8 FRESH SAGE LEAVES

FINE SEA SALT

FRESHLY GROUND BLACK PEPPER

¼ CUP DRY WHITE WINE

2 LARGE EGG YOLKS

JUICE OF 1 LEMON

1 TABLESPOON CHOPPED FRESH FLAT-LEAF PARSLEY

GARGANELLI AND CHICKEN RAGOUT WITH SAFFRON

SERVES 6 AS AN APPETIZER OR 4 AS A PASTA

IL CLASSICO

Saffron and leeks were a popular combination during the Renaissance.

LA MIA VERSIONE

This recipe, a simple ragout, uses leeks and saffron to create a new dish that tastes as though it might have been created in Florence centuries ago, although garganelli—the pasta twists—originated in Romagna.

⅓ CUP EXTRA VIRGIN OLIVE OIL

2 LEEKS, WHITE PARTS ONLY, RINSED AND THINLY SLICED

½ CUP VEGETABLE STOCK

2 PINCHES OF SAFFRON THREADS

1½ CUPS CHICKEN BREAST IN ⅛-INCH DICE

⅓ CUP DRY WHITE WINE

FINE SEA SALT

FRESHLY GROUND BLACK PEPPER

ONE 7-INCH-LONG NARROW ZUCCHINI, SLICED ⅛ INCH THICK LENGTHWISE, AND THEN CUT INTO ⅛-INCH DICE

1 TABLESPOON CHOPPED FRESH FLAT-LEAF PARSLEY

¾ POUND GARGANELLI

1 TABLESPOON UNSALTED BUTTER

⅓ CUP FRESHLY GRATED PARMIGIANO-REGGIANO, PLUS MORE FOR GARNISH IF DESIRED

1 Warm half the olive oil in a skillet over medium heat. Add the leeks and sauté until translucent, about 3 minutes.

2 Warm the stock in a deep skillet over medium heat. Add the saffron and let it dissolve.

3 Add the chicken to the skillet with the leeks and cook until golden, about 5 minutes. Sprinkle with the wine and let it evaporate, about 1 minute. Add the saffron broth, season with salt and pepper, and cook for 6 to 7 minutes.

4 Wipe the skillet used to dissolve the saffron. Add the rest of the oil and set over medium heat. Add the zucchini and sauté until golden-brown and crispy, about 5 minutes. Season with salt and pepper and add the parsley. Add the zucchini to the pan with the chicken and cook for 3 to 4 more minutes, until everything is amalgamated.

5 Set a large pot of salted water over high heat and bring to a boil. Add the garganelli and cook until al dente, about 7 minutes.

6 Drain the pasta, reserving some cooking water to add to the pasta in case the sauce becomes too dry. Add the drained pasta to the pan with the sauce and add the butter and Parmigiano. Mix thoroughly, adding some more cooking water if necessary. Top with extra Parmigiano if desired.

VINO A light Pinot Grigio from Friuli pairs nicely with the vegetables here.

RIGATONI WITH CHICKEN, PEAS, AND PROSCIUTTO

SERVES 6 AS AN APPETIZER OR 4 AS A MAIN COURSE

IL CLASSICO

Peas and diced prosciutto are a time-honored Tuscan side dish, traditionally served with veal, pork, and other meats.

LA MIA VERSIONE

In this dish, peas and diced prosciutto become the defining ingredients of a pasta sauce. I use rigatoni here, but it would also be delicious with fresh fettuccine or tagliarini. Be sure to top all of these with grated Parmigiano-Reggiano.

1 Warm half the olive oil in a sauté pan over medium heat. Add the scallions and cook them until translucent, about 3 minutes. Add the prosciutto and combine thoroughly with the scallions.

2 Warm the remaining olive oil in a skillet over medium-high heat. Add the chicken, season with salt and pepper, cook until browned, about 10 minutes, and stir into the pan with the scallions and prosciutto.

3 Raise the heat, add the wine, and cook until evaporated, about 1 minute. Lower the heat and add the peas, stock, and basil. Taste and add salt and pepper if necessary. Raise the heat and bring to a boil, then lower the heat and simmer for 5 minutes.

4 Meanwhile, bring a pot of salted water to a boil. Add the rigatoni and cook until al dente, about 10 minutes. Drain.

5 Remove the sauce from the heat and toss with the rigatoni. Top with the parsley just before serving and pass the Parmigiano at the table.

VINO Enjoy this rustic sauce with a young, full-bodied Chianti from Tuscany.

¼ CUP EXTRA VIRGIN OLIVE OIL

1 BUNCH SCALLIONS, BOTH WHITE AND GREEN PARTS, VERY THINLY SLICED

1 CUP PROSCIUTTO IN ⅛-INCH DICE

1 WHOLE CHICKEN BREAST, CUT INTO ⅛-INCH DICE

FINE SEA SALT

FRESHLY GROUND BLACK PEPPER

¼ CUP DRY WHITE WINE

2 CUPS PEAS, FRESH OR FROZEN

½ CUP VEGETABLE OR CHICKEN STOCK, SIMMERING IN A SMALL POT ON A BACK BURNER

4 FRESH BASIL LEAVES, TORN BY HAND

1 POUND RIGATONI

1 TABLESPOON CHOPPED FRESH FLAT-LEAF PARSLEY LEAVES

GRATED PARMIGIANO-REGGIANO FOR SERVING

BABY CHICKEN STEW SERVED IN A CROCK WITH A BREAD CRUST

———

SERVES 4 AS A MAIN COURSE

IL CLASSICO

La scarpetta (little shoe) is what Italians call the piece of bread used to soak up the last drops of a soup or sauce.

LA MIA VERSIONE

This recipe makes the scarpetta part of the dish by baking a bread crust over the crock itself. Use poussins if you can find them, but Rock Cornish game hens are an acceptable substitute.

To make this dish, you will need 4 crocks, each about 5 inches wide and 3 inches deep (the shape is not important). Alternately, you can make the dish in one large casserole, but be sure to spread the dough evenly over the top.

BREAD CRUST

¾ OUNCE FRESH YEAST

1½ CUPS WARM WATER

4 CUPS DURUM FLOUR (SEE IN SEARCH OF . . . , PAGE 16) OR ALL-PURPOSE FLOUR, PLUS MORE FOR DUSTING THE WORK SURFACE

2 TEASPOONS FINE SEA SALT

1 TO 2 TABLESPOONS FRESH MARJORAM LEAVES

¼ CUP EXTRA VIRGIN OLIVE OIL

1 Dissolve the yeast in a bowl with half the water. Put the flour on a clean work surface and make a well in the center. Pour the salt, yeast mixture, marjoram, and olive oil into the well. Use a fork to work the other ingredients into the flour and begin kneading it as soon as the ingredients are amalgamated. Add more water as needed to make a dough that is homogenous and elastic.

2 Dust a bowl roughly double the size of the dough with flour and place the dough in the bowl. Cover with plastic wrap and set it in a warm place to proof for about 2 hours. Meanwhile, make the chicken and artichokes.

(continued)

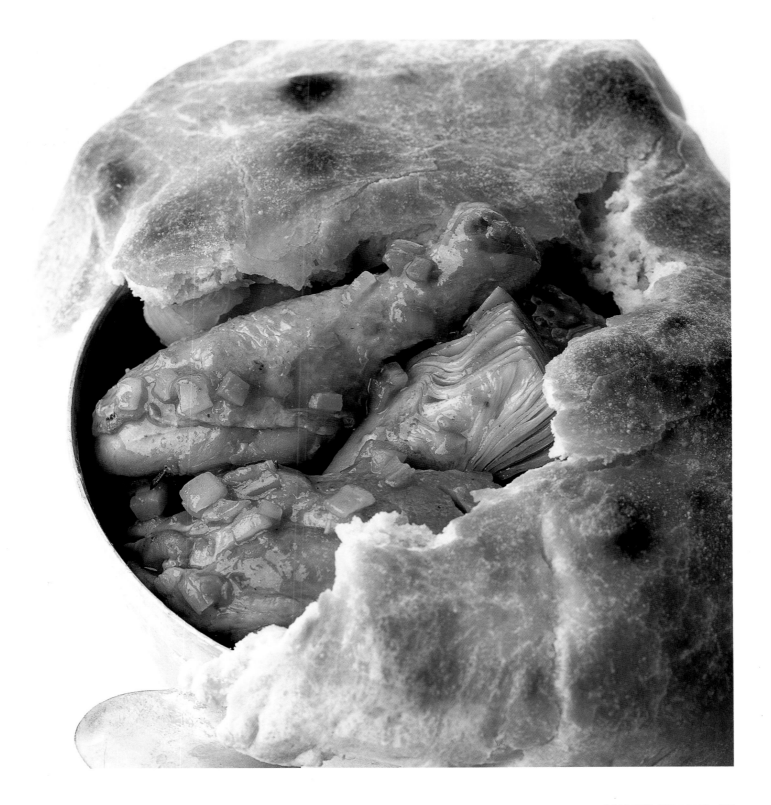

ABOUT ½ CUP EXTRA VIRGIN OLIVE OIL

½ CUP CHOPPED ONION

¼ CUP CHOPPED CARROT

¼ CUP CHOPPED CELERY

4 GARLIC CLOVES, MINCED

**FOUR 1-POUND BABY CHICKENS, CUT INTO
8 PIECES EACH**

FINE SEA SALT

FRESHLY GROUND BLACK PEPPER

½ CUP RED WINE VINEGAR

2 CUPS DRY WHITE WINE

2 CUPS CHICKEN STOCK

8 FRESH MARJORAM SPRIGS

**8 BABY ARTICHOKES, OUTER LEAVES REMOVED, TIPS
TRIMMED, EACH CUT INTO 6 WEDGES AND DROPPED
INTO COLD WATER MIXED WITH THE JUICE OF 1 LEMON**

¼ CUP EXTRA VIRGIN OLIVE OIL

1 TABLESPOON CHOPPED SHALLOT

8 FRESH MARJORAM SPRIGS

FINE SEA SALT

FRESHLY GROUND BLACK PEPPER

¼ CUP DRY WHITE WINE

¼ CUP VEGETABLE OR CHICKEN STOCK

CHICKEN

1 Warm half the olive oil in a large flameproof casserole over medium heat. Add the onion, carrot, celery, and garlic and sauté until the onion is translucent, about 5 minutes.

2 Meanwhile, pour the remaining olive oil into a large skillet and warm it over medium-high heat. Working in batches, add the chicken in a single layer without crowding and brown it on all sides, about 6 minutes per batch. Season with salt and pepper as it cooks, and add more oil between batches if necessary.

3 Transfer the browned chicken to the casserole with the vegetables and stir. Raise the heat to high and add the vinegar. Cook until it evaporates, about 3 minutes, then add the wine. When the wine has reduced by a little more than half, after about 10 minutes, add the stock and marjoram. Cover with a lid, lower the heat, and simmer until the chicken is tender and juicy, about 25 minutes. Meanwhile, cook the artichokes.

ARTICHOKES

Drain the artichokes and pat them dry with paper towels. Warm the olive oil in a sauté pan over medium heat. Add the shallot, sauté for 2 to 3 minutes, then stir in the artichokes and marjoram and season with salt and pepper. Add the wine and, when it has evaporated, after about 1 minute, the stock. Reduce the heat and cook for 5 more minutes, then remove from the heat.

ASSEMBLY

1 Preheat the oven to 350°F. When the dough has doubled in volume, turn it out onto a flour-dusted work surface and knead it until very smooth. Divide it into 4 parts and roll them, one at a time, with a rolling pin to form a circle about 7 inches in diameter.

2 Use tongs to pick out and discard the marjoram sprigs from the chicken casserole. Divide the baby chicken and its juice among the crocks, add the artichokes, brush the edges of the crocks with some water, and place the bread dough on top of each, carefully sealing it closed around the edges. Bake the crocks until the bread dough is golden and crusty, about 25 minutes. Serve in the crocks.

VINO Serve this dish with a young (and, if possible, dry) Dolcetto from Piemonte.

POLLO FRITTO ALLA TOSCANA

TUSCAN-STYLE FRIED CHICKEN

―――――――

SERVES 4 AS A MAIN COURSE

IL CLASSICO

In Florence they make fried chicken with a conventional batter of flour, water, and eggs. The same batter is often used to coat artichoke hearts, after which they are fried and served alongside the chicken.

LA MIA VERSIONE

This recipe marinates the chicken in garlic, lemon juice, and olive oil before coating it with flour. Feel free to make extra batter and fry artichokes, which are even better with this chicken than they are with the original.

1 Place the chicken pieces in a mixing bowl. Add the garlic, lemon juice, and olive oil. Season with black pepper and turn the pieces to coat thoroughly with the marinade. Cover and marinate in the refrigerator for 6 hours.

2 Remove the chicken pieces from the marinade and shake off the excess.

3 Break the eggs into a large bowl, beat them, and season with salt and pepper. Place the chicken pieces in the eggs, turn to coat, and leave them there for 1 hour.

4 Remove the chicken pieces from the eggs and dredge them in the flour.

5 Heat the vegetable oil until almost smoking in a deep pan set over medium heat, then add the chicken, a few pieces at a time, and cook until they are golden-brown and crispy, 5 to 7 minutes. As they are done, drain the pieces on paper towels, transfer to a platter, and keep them loosely covered with foil.

VINO Fried chicken demands something bold. My choice: Shiraz.

TWO 1-POUND POUSSINS OR CORNISH GAME HENS, CUT INTO 8 PIECES EACH

4 GARLIC CLOVES, SLICED

JUICE OF 2 LEMONS

½ CUP EXTRA VIRGIN OLIVE OIL

FRESHLY GROUND BLACK PEPPER

4 LARGE EGGS

FINE SEA SALT

1 CUP DURUM FLOUR (SEE IN SEARCH OF . . . , PAGE 16) OR ALL-PURPOSE FLOUR

6 CUPS VEGETABLE OIL

SPICY CORNISH HEN

———

SERVES 4 AS A MAIN COURSE

IL CLASSICO

Tuscan dishes cooked alla diavola ("devil's style") are very spicy with lots of black pepper and/or chiles.

LA MIA VERSIONE

This recipe, which borrows the Tuscan technique of chicken cooked under a brick, uses jalapeño for its heat, adding a distinctly south-of-the-border flavor.

FOUR 1-POUND CORNISH HENS, BUTTERFLIED, BREASTS BONED

1 GARLIC CLOVE, PEELED, PLUS 4 CLOVES, PEELED AND THINLY SLICED

1 TABLESPOON PLUS 1 TEASPOON HOT RED PEPPER FLAKES

FRESHLY GROUND BLACK PEPPER

JUICE OF 6 LEMONS

1 CUP EXTRA VIRGIN OLIVE OIL

2 FRESH ROSEMARY SPRIGS

4 FRESH THYME SPRIGS

1 JALAPEÑO PEPPER, SPLIT LENGTHWISE, SEEDS REMOVED, THINLY SLICED

FINE SEA SALT

1 Rub the Cornish hens' skin, inside and out, with the peeled garlic clove. Discard the clove. Spread the red pepper between the skin and the meat. Season all over with black pepper.

2 Place the hens in a nonreactive pan. Drizzle the lemon juice and olive oil over them then scatter the sliced garlic, rosemary, thyme, and jalapeño over them. Cover the pan with plastic wrap and let rest in the refrigerator overnight.

3 The next day, remove the hens from the marinade, pat them dry, and season the skins with salt.

4 Set a heavy cast-iron skillet large enough to fit all the hens (or use 2 or more smaller skillets) over medium heat. Place the hens, skin side down, in the skillet and press them with a spatula or weight (such as a cast-iron pan or foil-wrapped brick) to obtain a golden-brown crispy skin, then turn them over and repeat. Depending on the size of the hens, this will take 25 to 30 minutes altogether.

5 Place each hen on a dinner plate and serve at once.

VINO This spicy dish requires something that can stand up to its spice, like a full-bodied Brunello di Montalcino from Tuscany.

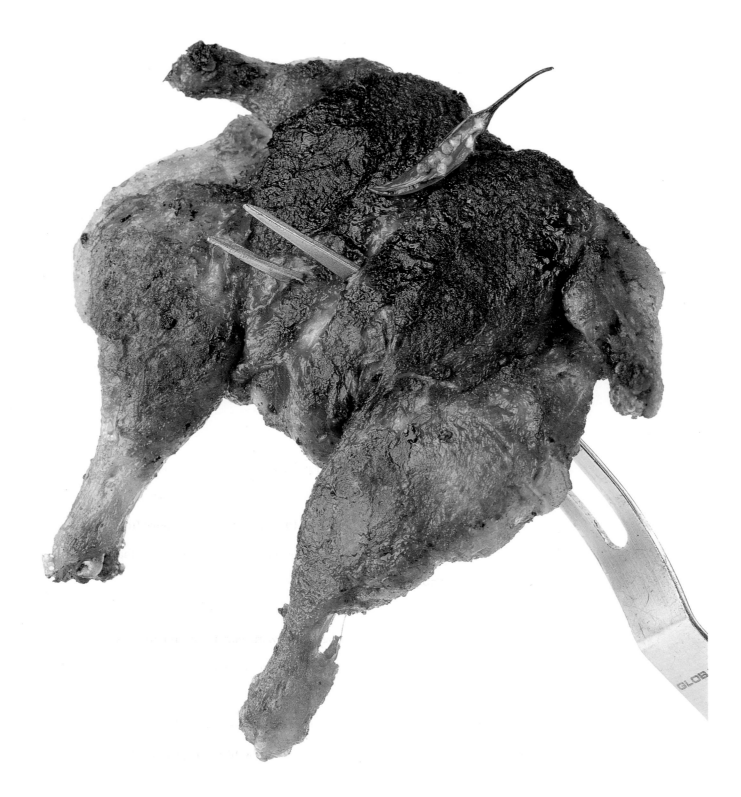

MAIALE
PORK

Tuscans love everything made from pork. When I was a child, my father had an annual ritual. He raised a pig. No, not pigs. He wasn't a farmer, though he enlisted one to care for his prized animal from summer through fall. He fed it and fattened it up, then—come January—he butchered it. From that pig we got pork chops, pork shoulder, pork loin, pancetta, and so on.

For this reason my palate associates pork with winter—for my formative years, we simply never had it at any other time. So in this chapter most of the dishes lean toward winter, such as Pork Stew with Winter Vegetables; Grilled Pork Chops with Roasted Pears and Pear Mustard, and Pork Chops Stuffed with Mortadella, Fontina, and Sage.

But there was an exception to the winter-only pork rule in our house: sausages and the cold cuts we made from them. Salami, prosciutto, mortadella, and soppressata are some of the most beloved of all Italian foods. We can't get enough of them. We devour them at breakfast, before lunch and dinner, and even between meals. When a Tuscan raids his refrigerator, he's looking for something that comes from a pig. It has such a natural affinity for our other staples—bread and olive oil—that we crave them all the time.

So, in this chapter there are also a number of dishes that draw on cold cuts such as Salami with Cherries, Prosciutto with Roasted Pears, and Prosciutto and Baked Pear Salad with Balsamic Vinegar.

There is one warm-weather dish that uses pork spareribs, Rostinciana in Umido, my Tuscan answer to American barbecued ribs. It's not here to challenge the American tradition of the barbecue but rather to offer an easier, indoor recipe that produces the same succulent result—a way to cook ribs even in the coldest winter weather, which is when I want to eat them.

SALAME NOSTRANO TOSCANO CON CILIEGE

SALAMI WITH CHERRIES

———

SERVES AS MANY AS YOU LIKE AS AN APPETIZER

IL CLASSICO

A few years ago I was visiting Delfina, a small village near Florence, where a restaurant served me cherries and salami—a perfect combination of sweet and salty flavors that I had never encountered before and a fine example of how the simplest classic can seem new and exciting.

LA MIA VERSIONE

To be perfectly honest, this recipe is the classic presentation, but it will be new to everyone reading this book. It's a wonderful way to begin a late spring or early summer meal. Be sure to purchase the leanest salami possible.

This is a very flexible recipe that will serve as many people as you like. Just add salami, cherries, and bread as you need them.

1 TUSCAN-STYLE SALAMI

FRESH SWEET CHERRIES

1 LOAF TUSCAN COUNTRY BREAD

Remove the skin from the salami and cut it into very thin slices. Serve it with the cherries and slices of bread. Encourage your guests to eat slices of cherries and salami together and alternate them with pieces of bread to refresh the palate.

IN SEARCH OF . . . TUSCAN SALAMI

Salame Toscano, or Tuscan salami, is an aged salami, usually 4 or 5 inches in diameter and 12 to 18 inches long. While it's rare here, very similar versions are produced in the United States under the names cacciatorini or just salami. Look for lots of marbleization and black peppercorns in the meat.

VINO Serve this with the favorite red wine of the farmers of southern Tuscany, a very dry Morellino.

PROSCIUTTO CON PERE ARROSTITE

PROSCIUTTO WITH ROASTED PEARS

——————

SERVES AS MANY AS YOU LIKE AS AN APPETIZER

IL CLASSICO

Pears are not a fruit one associates with the Italian palate, but when they're at their peak of freshness, their sweet flavor is a perfect accompaniment to prosciutto.

LA MIA VERSIONE

The novelty here is that the pears are *roasted,* which concentrates their flavor, caramelizes their natural sugar, and adds a smoky flavor that complements the prosciutto.

1 FIRM BOSC PEAR PER PERSON

1 TEASPOON GROUND CINNAMON FOR EVERY 4 PEARS

1 TEASPOON FRESHLY GRATED NUTMEG FOR EVERY 4 PEARS

1 TEASPOON GROUND GINGER FOR EVERY 4 PEARS

1 TEASPOON GROUND CARDAMOM FOR EVERY 4 PEARS

1 TO 2 THIN SLICES PROSCIUTTO DI PARMA OR TOSCANO PER PERSON

1 Preheat the oven to 200°F.

2 Cut the pears in half lengthwise. Remove the core, then cut each half in half lengthwise. Place them on a cookie sheet, skin side down.

3 In a mixing bowl, stir together the cinnamon, nutmeg, ginger, and cardamom. Transfer the spice mixture to a strainer and lightly dust the pears.

4 Place the cookie sheet in the oven and roast the pears until caramelized, about 45 minutes.

5 Serve the caramelized pears with the prosciutto.

VINO Serve this with a dry Prosecco from the Veneto, well chilled.

SAUTÉED "CARPACCIO" OF PORK IN A SPICY DANDELION SAUCE

SERVES 6 AS AN APPETIZER

IL CLASSICO

Salsa verde, a popular condiment throughout Italy best known as the classic accompaniment to bollito misto, is actually a catchall name for a family of sauces based on minced parsley. If fish is the ingredient to be enhanced, lemon juice is added; if it's meat, vinegar provides the acid and garlic, and mustard and bread cubes are added for greater depth of flavor.

LA MIA VERSIONE

In this dish bitter dandelion greens replace parsley for a distinctive and original salsa verde. It makes an especially profound impact because pork is so delicate, and all the more so when presented in carpaccio form. In many ways the meat in this dish is a tasty vehicle for the sauce rather than the sauce being a mere dressing for the meat.

1 CUP EXTRA VIRGIN OLIVE OIL

2 GARLIC CLOVES, PEELED

1½ POUNDS BONELESS PORK LOIN

FINE SEA SALT

FRESHLY GROUND BLACK PEPPER

2 BAY LEAVES

1 CUP DRY WHITE WINE

2 TEASPOONS FRESH FLAT-LEAF PARSLEY

¼ CUP TENDER DANDELION GREENS, RINSED AND JULIENNED

4 CORNICHONS, DRAINED

1 TABLESPOON DRAINED CAPERS

2 TABLESPOONS PICKLED ONIONS

1 SHALLOT

1½ HARD-COOKED EGGS, PEELED

½ CUP RED WINE VINEGAR

1 Warm ¼ cup of the olive oil in a flameproof casserole over medium heat. Add the garlic and sauté until golden, about 3 minutes. Add the meat, season to taste with salt and pepper, and sauté until golden on all sides, about 15 minutes.

2 Add the bay leaves and wine. Cook until the wine evaporates, about 3 minutes, then cover and reduce the heat to low. Cook for about 25 minutes, until the pork is cooked on the outside and lightly pink on the inside. Remove from the casserole and let cool.

3 Place the parsley in the bowl of a food processor and add the dandelion greens, cornichons, capers, pickled onions, shallot, eggs, vinegar, and the rest of the olive oil. Pulse until the sauce is coarse but well blended.

4 Slice the meat ⅛ inch thick with a slicing machine or a very sharp chef's knife used as steadily as possible. To serve, arrange the slices in a circle on a serving platter or on individual plates and drizzle the sauce on top.

VINO A vintage Chianti from Tuscany will contrast nicely with the salsa verde.

SALSICCIA STUFATA CON CIPOLLE E PEPERONI
SAUSAGE, ONION, AND PEPPER STEW

___

SERVES 4 TO 6 AS AN APPETIZER

IL CLASSICO

This is a variation on a classic chicken dish in which onions and peppers are cooked over low heat until they begin to fall apart.

LA MIA VERSIONE

This recipe converts the classic one into a vehicle for sausage; it's especially delicious stirred into a cooked risotto.

7 ONIONS, THINLY SLICED

4 LARGE VINE-RIPENED TOMATOES, THINLY SLICED

1 RED BELL PEPPER, JULIENNED

1 YELLOW BELL PEPPER, JULIENNED

FINE SEA SALT

FRESHLY GROUND BLACK PEPPER

¼ CUP EXTRA VIRGIN OLIVE OIL

1½ POUNDS (ABOUT 6 LINKS) SWEET SAUSAGE

2 TABLESPOONS WHITE WINE VINEGAR

1 Place the onions in a wide shallow skillet and add the tomatoes and bell peppers. Season with salt and pepper and pour the olive oil on top.

2 Set the skillet over low heat and cook, stirring occasionally, until the vegetables are very soft, 20 to 25 minutes.

3 In the meantime, prick the sausages with a fork, then place them in a sauté pan. Add ¼ cup water, cover, and cook over medium heat for about 10 minutes, until the fat is rendered.

4 Add the sausages to the vegetables and cook for another 15 minutes. Add the vinegar, stir well, and cook for another 5 minutes. Divide among individual plates and serve.

VINO I suggest Sfurzat, a red wine from Italy's northeasternmost region, Friuli-Venezia-Giulia.

PROSCIUTTO AND BAKED PEAR SALAD WITH BALSAMIC VINEGAR

———

SERVES 4 AS AN APPETIZER

IL CLASSICO

Prosciutto and figs or melon are a classic Italian pairing.

LA MIA VERSIONE

A knife-and-fork version of a famous hors d'oeuvre.

2 LARGE RIPE PEARS

1 TABLESPOON PLUS 1 TEASPOON RAW BROWN SUGAR (TURBINADO)

¼ TEASPOON GROUND CINNAMON

¼ TEASPOON GROUND GINGER

¼ TEASPOON FRESHLY GRATED NUTMEG

5 OUNCES MÂCHE, RINSED AND SPUN DRY

FINE SEA SALT

1 TEASPOON ACETO BALSAMICO TRADIZIONALE DI MODENA

1 TABLESPOON EXTRA VIRGIN OLIVE OIL

16 THIN SLICES PROSCIUTTO DI PARMA

1 Preheat the oven to 300°F.

2 Rinse the pears and trim off stems. Halve, core, and cut each pear into 6 wedges.

3 In a bowl, stir together the sugar, cinnamon, ginger, and nutmeg.

4 Line a rimmed cookie sheet with parchment paper and arrange the pears, skin side down, in a single layer over the paper. Sprinkle the spice mixture over them; cover tightly with aluminum foil and bake for 40 minutes. Remove the foil and continue to bake until the pears are caramelized, 30 to 40 more minutes. Remove the cookie sheet from the oven and allow the pears to cool until warm.

5 Meanwhile, place the mâche in a salad bowl. In a separate small bowl, use a whisk to dissolve ¼ teaspoon salt in the vinegar and, whisking continuously, add the oil. Pour the vinaigrette over the salad and toss well.

6 Divide the prosciutto, caramelized pears, and dressed greens among 4 salad plates and serve at once.

IN SEARCH OF . . . ACETO BALSAMICO TRADIZIONALE DI MODENA
Though there are many weak imitations sold as balsamic vinegar, true balsamic hails from one place only: Modena. It is very expensive, but in dishes like this, and the cheese plate on page 240, its intensity and complexity are worth every penny.

VINO A slightly chilled, sparkling red Barbera will offset the sweetness of the pears and the saltiness of the prosciutto.

ORECCHIETTE WITH DANDELION, SAUSAGE, AND LEMON ZEST

———

SERVES 6 AS AN APPETIZER OR 4 AS A MAIN COURSE

IL CLASSICO

The classic accompaniment to orecchiette (ear-shaped pasta) is bitter broccoli rabe and spicy sausage. The dish originated in the Apulia region, where pasta is made with water instead of egg, which yields a chewy pasta that pairs well with such assertively flavored ingredients.

LA MIA VERSIONE

In this recipe the broccoli rabe has been replaced by sautéed dandelion greens for bitterness (orecchiette has a great affinity for bitterness, which includes the slightly bitter extra virgin olive oil from Puglia). The lemon zest emphasizes the bitterness, and its acidity cuts the sausage's fat.

FINE SEA SALT

1½ POUNDS DANDELION GREENS, TOUGH OUTER LEAVES REMOVED, RINSED, AND SLICED 1 INCH THICK

¼ CUP EXTRA VIRGIN OLIVE OIL

2 GARLIC CLOVES, CRUSHED

2 PINCHES OF HOT RED PEPPER FLAKES

GRATED ZEST OF 1 LEMON

1½ CUPS CRUMBLED HOT SAUSAGE MEAT

½ CUP DRY WHITE WINE

1 POUND ORECCHIETTE

⅓ CUP GRATED PECORINO ROMANO

FRESHLY GROUND BLACK PEPPER

1 Bring a pot of salted water to a boil over high heat. Add the dandelion greens to the pot and cook, stirring, for 5 minutes. Drain.

2 Heat the olive oil in a sauté pan over medium-high heat. Add the garlic and sauté until browned, about 2 minutes. Remove the garlic from the pan and discard it. Add the cooked dandelion greens to the pan, stirring to coat them with the oil. Season with salt, red pepper, and lemon zest. Cover with a lid and lower the heat. Cook for about 20 minutes or until the vegetables are tender.

3 Place the sausage meat in a large skillet over low heat. Cook until the fat begins to render. Raise the heat and add the wine to the pan. Cook until the alcohol evaporates, about 3 minutes, then add the dandelion greens, stir, and cook over low heat for 10 minutes.

4 Meanwhile, bring another pot of salted water to a boil and cook the orecchiette until al dente, about 7 minutes. Reserve ½ cup of the pasta cooking liquid and drain the pasta. Transfer it to a big bowl and add the sauce, mixing as you do. Add a bit of cooking liquid to help it emulsify. Finish by topping with grated Pecorino Romano and black pepper and serve family style at the table.

VINO The potent flavors of sausage and dandelion greens demand a full-bodied California Cabernet.

PORK IN GRAPE SAUCE

———

SERVES 6 AS A MAIN COURSE

IL CLASSICO

Generations ago, agresto was a tartly flavored meat and seafood condiment commonly made from the reduced juice of unripened grapes. It was invented to assuage the frustration of Tuscan winemakers looking for an alternative to discarding the July grapes they cut every year to strengthen the vines. There are several theories about the origin of the word *agresto*; I think it must come from the Latin word *acer*, which means "sharp." (American wine cognoscenti might recognize it as an ancestor of verjus.) Once a very popular source of acidity in numerous recipes, it has been replaced by more practical and accessible alternatives like a squeeze of lemon.

LA MIA VERSIONE

This is actually a very traditional recipe, which seems new today because virtually no contemporary diner has ever tasted (or heard of) agresto.

Serve this with the Roasted Autumn Vegetable Salad on page 111.

---

5 POUNDS WHITE GRAPES OR 1 CUP VERJUS

4 CELERY RIBS, SLICED ¼ INCH THICK

1 MEDIUM ONION, CUT INTO SMALL DICE

½ CUP FRESH SAGE LEAVES

2 FRESH ROSEMARY SPRIGS

2 CUPS DRY WHITE WINE

10 GARLIC CLOVES, THINLY SLICED

2 POUNDS RACK OF PORK ON THE BONE, CHINE OFF

FINE SEA SALT

FRESHLY GROUND BLACK PEPPER

¼ POUND PANCETTA, THINLY SLICED

¼ CUP EXTRA VIRGIN OLIVE OIL

2 BAY LEAVES

(continued)

1 If you're using grapes, place them along with the celery, onion, sage, rosemary, wine, and 8 of the garlic cloves in a pot and set over low heat. Add 2 cups water and reduce the liquid gradually until almost dry over 1 hour, stirring periodically. Remove from the heat, let cool, and process in a blender or food processor. The mixture should be very liquid. (Skip this step if using verjus.)

2 Place the pork in a stainless-steel pan and pour the grape mixture or verjus over it. Cover with plastic wrap and marinate for a couple of hours, turning the meat on all sides.

3 Remove the pork from the marinade, pat it dry with paper towels, and season it all over with salt and pepper. Set the grape juice aside. Wrap the meat with pancetta and tie it in several places with kitchen string.

4 Heat the olive oil in a flameproof casserole set over medium heat. Add the remaining garlic and sauté until browned, about 4 minutes. Add the meat and cook, turning it as the pancetta browns and basting with the marinade, until the pancetta is brown and crispy on all sides, about 20 minutes altogether.

5 Add the reserved reduced grape juice and the bay leaves, and cook uncovered for 5 minutes. Cover and cook for about 1 hour, until, when you prick the meat with a skewer, the meat is tender and the juices run clear. If the liquid begins to dry up in the pan, add some water.

6 Serve the meat on a cutting board and slice it at the table, pouring the sauce over the slices.

VINO A good-vintage Barolo, preferably a reserve, will provide a stark red contrast to the white wine–themed sauce, as will a Dolcetto.

ROSTINCIANA IN UMIDO

PORK SPARERIBS, TUSCAN STYLE

———

SERVES 6 AS A MAIN COURSE

IL CLASSICO

In umido is a Tuscan phrase that means to braise fish or meat in a scant quantity of liquid, usually tomato sauce with wine and/or stock.

LA MIA VERSIONE

You probably think of spareribs as a barbecue affair, but we've devised a way of cooking them in umido that produces a more "wet," succulent dish with tangy flavor that doesn't require an outdoor grill. Serve this with the Roasted Autumn Vegetable Salad (page 111) or sautéed dandelion greens.

---

1 Pour the olive oil into a sauté pan wide and deep enough to hold all the ribs. Place over medium heat. When the oil is hot, add the ribs in a single layer and brown them slowly, turning until all sides are browned.

2 Transfer the ribs to a plate and set aside.

3 To the same pan, add the onion and parsley and cook until the onion is translucent, about 5 minutes, then add the garlic, cinnamon, cloves, and black pepper. Return the ribs to the pan and move them around with tongs to let them absorb the flavor and the heat.

4 Pour the wine into the pan and scrape the bottom of the pan with a wooden spoon to loosen any flavorful bits. Cook until the wine has evaporated, about 2 minutes, then add the tomatoes and their liquid. Cover with a lid and simmer for about 1½ hours, until the meat is tender and the sauce is reduced to a creamy consistency. Season with salt and serve from a platter or on individual plates.

VINO Pair this with a fruity young Tuscan Merlot.

3 TABLESPOONS EXTRA VIRGIN OLIVE OIL

5 POUNDS PORK SPARERIBS, SEPARATED INTO INDIVIDUAL RIBS, EXCESS FAT TRIMMED

1 LARGE ONION, FINELY CHOPPED

¼ CUP CHOPPED FRESH FLAT-LEAF PARSLEY

2 GARLIC CLOVES, CHOPPED

PINCH OF GROUND CINNAMON

SCANT PINCH OF GROUND CLOVES

¼ TEASPOON FRESHLY GROUND BLACK PEPPER

1 CUP RED WINE

TWO 16-OUNCE CANS WHOLE TOMATOES IN THEIR JUICE, CRUSHED BY HAND

FINE SEA SALT

PORK STEW WITH WINTER VEGETABLES

———

SERVES 4 TO 6 AS A MAIN COURSE

IL CLASSICO

Spezzatino, which means "diced and stewed," is a stew of cubed veal shoulder or shank that is also made sometimes with chicken or lamb.

LA MIA VERSIONE

Here the recipe has been adapted to use pork and expanded through the addition of cubes of butternut squash, turnip, and celery root. The most dramatic adjustment actually isn't the pork but the addition of quince, one of the most fragrant fruits of the season. It is a fruit that has been used since medieval times, at least, and gives an unusual yet classic spin to this dish.

———

⅓ CUP EXTRA VIRGIN OLIVE OIL

¼ CUP CHOPPED CARROT

¼ CUP CHOPPED CELERY

½ CUP CHOPPED ONION

1½ POUNDS BONELESS PORK FROM THE LEG OR SHOULDER, TRIMMED
AND CUT INTO 1½-INCH CUBES

FINE SEA SALT

FRESHLY GROUND BLACK PEPPER

1 CUP DRY WHITE WINE

1 CUP VEGETABLE OR CHICKEN STOCK

1 HERB SACHET: 1 BAY LEAF, 2 FRESH ROSEMARY SPRIGS, 4 FRESH SAGE LEAVES, 3 GARLIC
CLOVES, AND 1 TEASPOON BLACK PEPPERCORNS TIED IN A CHEESECLOTH BUNDLE

1½ CUPS PEELED CELERY ROOT IN 1-INCH CUBES

1½ CUPS PEELED TURNIP IN 1-INCH CUBES

1½ CUPS PEELED AND SEEDED BUTTERNUT SQUASH IN 1-INCH CUBES

1½ CUPS PEELED QUINCE IN 1-INCH DICE

1 Pour half the olive oil into a flameproof casserole over low heat. Add the carrot, celery, and onion and sauté until the onion is translucent, about 20 minutes.

2 Warm the rest of the olive oil in a skillet over medium-high heat. Add the meat a little at a time, seasoning it with salt and pepper and searing it, about 4 minutes altogether.

3 Transfer the browned meat to the casserole, stirring well, and cook for 5 minutes. Increase the heat to high and add the wine.

4 When the wine has reduced by half, after about 2 minutes, add the stock and herb sachet. Reduce the heat to low, add the celery root, and cover. After 20 minutes, add the turnip. After another 10 minutes, add the butternut squash and quince. Taste and adjust the seasoning if necessary.

5 Cook for 30 more minutes, then prick the meat with a knife. If it is tender, remove the casserole from the stove; otherwise, cook a bit more, adding a small amount of hot water if it becomes too dry.

6 To serve, divide the stew among individual plates.

VINO This great winter dish requires a great red Burgundy or a Sonoma Pinot Noir.

PORK TENDERLOIN STUFFED WITH CHICKEN LIVER PÂTÉ

SERVES 4 AS A MAIN COURSE

IL CLASSICO

Beef Wellington is a classic English dish in which beef tenderloin is spread with foie gras and mushrooms, then wrapped in pastry and baked.

LA MIA VERSIONE

This recipe makes an Italian dish by substituting pork tenderloin for the beef and substituting a mixture of chicken liver and herbs for the foie gras. The addition of prosciutto is a further Italian touch. Serve this with roasted acorn squash.

CHICKEN LIVER PÂTÉ

½ POUND CHICKEN LIVERS, RINSED

½ CUP MARSALA

2 TABLESPOONS UNSALTED BUTTER

2 TABLESPOONS MINCED SHALLOT

4 FRESH SAGE LEAVES, TORN BY HAND

FINE SEA SALT

FRESHLY GROUND BLACK PEPPER

1 Soak the livers in the Marsala for 4 to 5 hours. Strain over a bowl and reserve the livers and wine separately.

2 Melt 1 tablespoon of the butter in a sauté pan over medium-high heat. Add the shallot and sauté until translucent, about 2 minutes. Add the chicken livers and sage and season with salt and pepper. Sauté for about 5 minutes, then add ¼ cup of the reserved Marsala wine. Cook for about 1 minute to let the alcohol evaporate, then remove the pan from the heat.

3 Transfer the livers to the bowl of a food processor fitted with the metal blade. Add the remaining butter and pulse. Add the remaining Marsala and process for 30 more seconds. Transfer the mixture to a bowl, cover, and refrigerate.

1 Heat the olive oil in a skillet over medium heat and brown the pork tenderloin, seasoning lightly with salt (being mindful that the prosciutto is salty) and pepper. Transfer the pork to a clean, dry work surface and let cool.

2 When the meat has cooled enough to handle, spread the chicken liver pâté evenly on the pork, about ⅛ inch thick, then wrap each tenderloin with the prosciutto.

3 Preheat the oven to 325°F.

4 On a flour-dusted work surface, roll the puff pastry out ⅛ inch thick and, with a pasta cutter, cut rectangles the right size to wrap each piece of pork tenderloin individually. Wrap the tenderloins, then place the meat on a cookie sheet lined with parchment paper.

5 In a small bowl, whisk together the egg yolk and milk. Brush the puff pastry with this wash. Bake the pork until the crust is golden, about 25 minutes. Place one tenderloin on each of 4 plates and serve at once.

VINO A full-bodied, good-vintage Brunello di Montalcino or Rosso di Montalcino can still make its presence known, even against the liver and Marsala.

¼ CUP EXTRA VIRGIN OLIVE OIL

FOUR ½-POUND PIECES PORK TENDERLOIN, TRIMMED OF FAT

FINE SEA SALT

FRESHLY GROUND BLACK PEPPER

¼ POUND PROSCIUTTO DI PARMA, VERY THINLY SLICED

1 POUND PUFF PASTRY, FRESH OR FROZEN

1 LARGE EGG YOLK

5 TABLESPOONS MILK

GRILLED PORK CHOPS WITH ROASTED PEARS AND PEAR MUSTARD

———

SERVES 4 AS A MAIN COURSE

IL CLASSICO

Traditionally, pork chops are roasted and served with simple accompaniments such as Swiss chard, broccoli rabe, mashed potatoes, or fruit mustard (a tangy fruit condiment, similar to chutney).

LA MIA VERSIONE

This dish takes pork chops to a whole new level by marinating them and grilling them, then pairing them with a trio of Tuscan-inspired side dishes: succulent roasted pears, tangy pear mustard, and sautéed bitter dandelion. (I suggest preparing a larger amount of pear mustard and placing it in well-sealed jars. It will last for up to two weeks stored in the refrigerator.) Note that the pears need to be started two days before you plan to serve the chops.

---

1 POUND PEARS, NOT TOO RIPE, PLUS 2 RIPE PEARS CUT INTO QUARTERS
WITH THE SKIN ON

¾ CUP GRANULATED SUGAR

⅛ TEASPOON MUSTARD POWDER

¼ TEASPOON GROUND CINNAMON

¼ TEASPOON GROUND GINGER

¼ TEASPOON FRESHLY GRATED NUTMEG

1 TABLESPOON PLUS 1 TEASPOON BROWN SUGAR

FINE SEA SALT

1 BUNCH DANDELION GREENS, TOUGH OUTER LEAVES REMOVED, RINSED,
AND SLICED 1 INCH THICK

¼ CUP EXTRA VIRGIN OLIVE OIL

4 GARLIC CLOVES, PEELED, 2 WHOLE AND 2 CRUSHED

2 PINCHES OF HOT RED PEPPER FLAKES

FRESHLY GROUND BLACK PEPPER

4 DOUBLE-CUT PORK CHOPS

4 FRESH ROSEMARY SPRIGS

1 Peel the pound of pears and cut each one into 8 wedges. Place them in a mixing bowl and sprinkle with the granulated sugar. Cover with plastic wrap, then let sit in the refrigerator for 24 hours.

2 Remove the pears from the refrigerator and pour the accumulated juice into a saucepan over medium heat. Cook until the liquid is reduced by half, about 5 minutes, then pour it over the pears, cover them, and refrigerate them for an additional 24 hours.

3 Remove the pears from the juice and place them in a nonstick pan. Set over medium heat and sauté until they start to caramelize, about 5 minutes. Add the juice and cook until the liquid is reduced by half, about 6 minutes.

4 Remove from the heat and let cool, then add the mustard powder. Place in a jar or bowl until ready to use.

5 Preheat the oven to 300°F.

6 In a mixing bowl, stir together the cinnamon, ginger, nutmeg, and brown sugar.

7 Place the quartered pears in a nonstick baking pan. Dust them with the spice mixture, then cover with aluminum foil. Bake for 30 minutes. Remove the foil and bake for 30 more minutes or until the pears are caramelized.

8 Set a pot of salted water over high heat and bring to a boil. Add the dandelion greens, stirring, and cook for about 5 minutes. Drain.

9 Warm the olive oil in a sauté pan set over medium heat. Add the crushed garlic cloves and sauté until browned, about 2 minutes. Remove and discard the garlic.

10 Add the dandelion greens to the pan, stirring, and add the red pepper. Season with salt and black pepper, cover, and reduce the heat to low. Cook for about 20 minutes, until the greens are tender.

(continued)

11 Rub the pork chops with the remaining 2 garlic cloves. Put 1 rosemary sprig on top of each chop and marinate them in the refrigerator for a couple of hours.

12 Light a fire in your outdoor grill or preheat your broiler. Cook the chops to desired doneness, turning to brown both sides. When you remove them from the fire, season with salt and black pepper.

13 Serve the grilled chops with the dandelion, the pears, and the pear mustard.

VINO Serve this with a full-bodied Merlot from California.

PORK CHOPS STUFFED WITH MORTADELLA, FONTINA, AND SAGE

———

SERVES 4 AS A MAIN COURSE

IL CLASSICO

The Valle d'Aosta is a region of northern Italy that abuts both France and Switzerland. Local cheeses, especially Fontina, are popular in the region's cuisine and a dish with Fontina melted over it is referred to as being cooked *alla valdostana*.

LA MIA VERSIONE

Here we expand on the notion of a pork chop alla valdostana, adding mortadella and sage and stuffing the pork chop rather than topping it. Serve this with whole roasted shallots and mashed potatoes.

FOUR 1-POUND PORK CHOPS

4 THIN SLICES FONTINA

2 THIN SLICES MORTADELLA

12 FRESH SAGE LEAVES

¼ CUP EXTRA VIRGIN OLIVE OIL

2 GARLIC CLOVES

FINE SEA SALT

FRESHLY GROUND BLACK PEPPER

1 CUP VIN SANTO

½ CUP VEGETABLE STOCK

1 Preheat the oven to 350°F.

2 With a very sharp knife, make a cut horizontally in the chops, creating a pocket.

3 Stuff each chop with 1 slice Fontina, ½ slice mortadella, and 1 sage leaf. Place 1 sage leaf on top of each chop, pressing tightly so it adheres.

4 Warm the olive oil in a flameproof casserole over medium heat. Add the garlic and sauté until browned, about 3 minutes, then remove and discard it. Add the chops in a single layer without crowding and cook slowly, turning once, until browned on both sides, about 20 minutes. Season with salt and pepper, then pour the Vin Santo into the casserole and add the remaining sage leaves. As the wine evaporates, which should take about 10 minutes, use a wooden spoon to scrape up any brown bits stuck to the bottom of the casserole.

5 Add the stock, cover with a lid or aluminum foil, and finish in the oven for 15 minutes. Divide among individual dinner plates, pouring the juice on top of the chops.

IN SEARCH OF . . . VIN SANTO

Vin Santo means "holy wine." It is a sweet dessert wine made from the juice of malvasia and trebbiano grapes that are dried and pressed, then aged for three years. It is powerfully flavored, not unlike a fortified wine.

VINO A South African Syrah is an unusual red wine that supports all these flavors.

In every town in Tuscany, there is an important man who does things that others would rather not know about. He labors alone, in dimly lit back rooms, away from the public eye. Everyone knows and respects the tasks he performs. And they all come to him, because he offers what no one else can provide. They darken the door of his place of business and tell him what they need, too polite to stare at the lingering evidence of his work, like his quickened breath, sweat-dappled brow, or the streak of fresh blood on his shirt. He listens to their requests, nods his comprehension of what he must do, then disappears through the back door to carry out their wishes.

This man is the town butcher, or *macellaio,* and he is as beloved and essential a figure as the local mayor, priest, or doctor.

Much has been written of Italian painters, sculptors, and architects; of the poets, novelists, and filmmakers of my native country. Even fashion designers and automobile manufacturers have attained fame and fortune.

But where is the praise for the butchers of Italy? The men who for centuries have perfected the craft, taught to them by their fathers and grandfathers, of isolating the very specific qualities of different cuts of beef, veal, and lamb and mastering the ability to remove those cuts in precise, artful strokes?

A great butcher is a clairvoyant. When he sets to work on the carcass of a veal laid out on his table, he sees the future. Removing the scaloppine, he envisions them pounded out, quickly sautéed, and dressed with creamy sauce poured over them from the hot pan. Carving the breast, he imagines it seared in a skillet and transferred to the fiery confines of an oven, where it roasts with herbs and potato wedges. Turning his attention to the leg, he sees a long-simmered osso buco being removed from a cauldron with tongs and perched atop a yellow-tinged risotto Milanese.

The butcher is no less essential a figure in your culinary life than the farmers and grocers from whom you buy your other ingredients. And, in my humble opinion, respect must be paid. (Though, it must be said, these men are well compensated, so much so that they all purchase the same car— a Mercedes 500!)

These recipes are inventive and unique, but they too depend on the talent of *your* local butcher. And this chapter is dedicated to the macellai of Italy, with thanks for their contribution to the gastronomy of our nation.

HOT STEAK SALAD WITH SLICED POTATO, HERBS, AND ONION

———

SERVES 4 AS A MAIN COURSE

IL CLASSICO

Bistecca Fiorentina is one of the classic Tuscan dishes, a thick steak (usually a T-bone) grilled to perfection and topped with olive oil and herbs, only after it's been cooked.

LA MIA VERSIONE

Here we take the concept of a grilled Florentine steak in a different direction by preparing an herbaceous dressing for the steak and making it the cornerstone of a main-dish summer salad.

You may want to wait until the steaks have marinated before making the dressing so its flavors are fresh and light.

DRESSING

10 FRESH BASIL LEAVES

10 FRESH MINT LEAVES

20 FRESH FLAT-LEAF PARSLEY LEAVES

LEAVES FROM 8 FRESH MARJORAM SPRIGS

LEAVES FROM 8 FRESH THYME SPRIGS

LEAVES FROM 8 FRESH OREGANO SPRIGS

1 GARLIC CLOVE, PEELED AND CRUSHED

1 TEASPOON FINE SEA SALT

⅓ CUP EXTRA VIRGIN OLIVE OIL

Place the herbs, garlic, and salt on a cutting board and chop them together finely. Transfer the mixture to a bowl. Gradually add the olive oil in a thin stream, whisking to form a well-integrated dressing. Set aside.

STEAK AND ASSEMBLY

1 In a small bowl, whisk together the crushed garlic, lemon juice, and half the olive oil until emulsified. Rub the meat with this marinade and let it marinate, covered, in the refrigerator, for 2 to 4 hours.

2 Place the potatoes, skin on, in a pot, cover with lightly salted water, and bring to a boil over high heat. Cook until tender but still firm, then use a slotted spoon to remove them from the water and let cool to room temperature. Peel the potatoes and slice into half-moon shapes about ¼ inch thick. Set aside.

3 Warm the rest of the olive oil in a skillet over medium-high heat. Add the tomatoes and basil and sauté for 2 to 3 minutes, seasoning with salt and pepper. Remove from the heat and set aside, covered, to keep warm.

4 Prepare an outdoor grill for cooking.

5 Pat the meat dry with a paper towel, then grill it to medium-rare. When it has cooled enough to handle it, slice it lengthwise at a 45-degree angle, ¼ inch thick.

6 Place the meat slices in a salad bowl and add the potatoes, cucumber, onions, and tomatoes; pour the dressing over the salad, season with salt and pepper, and toss thoroughly. Serve at once, either family style or from individual plates.

VINO A full-bodied reserve Chianti from Tuscany is a fine match for both the grilled steak and the salad vegetables.

---

1 GARLIC CLOVE, CRUSHED

JUICE OF ½ LEMON

1½ TEASPOONS EXTRA VIRGIN OLIVE OIL

2 NEW YORK STEAKS, ABOUT 1½ POUNDS EACH

4 MEDIUM YUKON GOLD POTATOES

FINE SEA SALT

4 RIPE BUT FIRM VINE-RIPENED TOMATOES, BLANCHED AND PEELED (SEE PAGE 25), CUT INTO WEDGES, SEEDS DISCARDED

4 FRESH BASIL LEAVES

FRESHLY GROUND BLACK PEPPER

½ ENGLISH CUCUMBER, PEELED AND JULIENNED

2 RED ONIONS, CUT IN HALF AND THINLY SLICED

VEAL RAGOUT WITH SAGE AND GARGANELLI

———

SERVES 6 AS AN APPETIZER OR 4 AS A PASTA

IL CLASSICO

Veal ragout is a popular dish in Italy, often served with a dried pasta that can absorb the strong flavor.

LA MIA VERSIONE

Garganelli is an unusual pasta selection for veal ragout, especially fresh garganelli. Its lightness and delicacy makes this an exceptionally elegant pasta dish, but you can use dried garganelli or fusilli with excellent results, too.

GARGANELLI

5½ CUPS DURUM FLOUR (SEE IN SEARCH OF . . . , PAGE 16) OR ALL-PURPOSE FLOUR

6 LARGE EGGS

SEMOLINA FLOUR FOR DUSTING COOKIE SHEET

1 Place the flour on a smooth, clean surface and make a well in the middle. Place the eggs in the well and mix them into the flour a little at a time with the help of a fork; then knead until the dough has a smooth and even consistency. Roll the dough through a pasta machine (or use a rolling pin) to make sheets about ⅛ inch thick.

2 Have ready a dowel about ¼ inch in diameter or a clean pencil and a butter paddle or a clean (preferably new) comb.

3 Working with a small amount of dough at time and keeping the pasta sheet covered with a damp towel or plastic wrap, cut the pasta into 1½-inch squares.

4 Place one square on the paddle or comb with a corner pointing toward you. Lay the dowel across the square of pasta and roll it so the opposite corners overlap and seal. Then roll the dowel over the paddle or comb to make grooves in the dough; slip the garganelli from the dowel and place on a towel-covered tray dusted with semolina flour. Set aside.

(continued)

2 TABLESPOONS UNSALTED BUTTER

¼ CUP EXTRA VIRGIN OLIVE OIL

1 CELERY RIB, CHOPPED

1 CARROT, CHOPPED

1 LARGE ONION, CHOPPED

1 POUND GROUND VEAL

1 CUP DRY WHITE WINE

8 FRESH SAGE LEAVES

1 TEASPOON FRESHLY GRATED NUTMEG

FINE SEA SALT

FRESHLY GROUND BLACK PEPPER

1 CUP CHICKEN STOCK

1 CUP WHOLE MILK

FRESHLY GRATED PARMIGIANO-REGGIANO FOR GARNISH

1 In a wide heavy flameproof casserole over medium-low heat, melt the butter with half the olive oil. Add the celery, carrot, and onion and sauté until golden, about 5 minutes, stirring occasionally.

2 Heat the rest of the olive oil in a skillet over medium-high heat and sear the meat in a single layer, a little bit at a time, then stir the meat into the casserole with the vegetables.

3 Add the wine, tear the sage leaves by hand and add them, then add the nutmeg. Season with salt and pepper. When the wine has evaporated, about 4 minutes, add half the chicken stock and the milk and simmer, covered, for 1 hour. (Check occasionally, adding more stock or water if the mixture begins to stick to the bottom of the pan.)

4 Meanwhile, bring a large pot of salted water to a boil and cook the garganelli until al dente, about 4 minutes, then drain and transfer to a serving bowl, adding the hot ragout. Top with Parmigiano and serve.

VINO If you make this dish in late fall, a Vino Novello from Tuscany is the right way to go. That or a Beaujolais Nouveau.

ORECCHIETTE WITH BEEF ROLL-UPS

IL CLASSICO

Involtini refers to stuffed rolls of meat or fish. It was created back when meat was scarce and southern Italians had to devise ways to make the most out of very little, in this case rolling a flattened slice of beef around a stuffing to give it the look of a small roast.

LA MIA VERSIONE

This pairing of hefty orecchiette in red sauce with rolled and tied slices of beef makes for a very filling meal. It's a variation on the classic involtini in humido, in which pasta is tossed in the same sauce as the birds.

---

1 Place each slice of beef between 2 pieces of plastic wrap and pound to a thickness of about ⅛ inch.

2 On top of each slice of beef, place 1 slice pancetta, 1 slice Pecorino Toscano, a quarter of the parsley, and a quarter of the garlic. Season to taste with salt and pepper, then roll up each slice and tie firmly at 1-inch intervals with kitchen string.

3 Warm the olive oil in a sauté pan set over medium heat. Add the onion and sauté until translucent, about 5 minutes. Arrange the meat in the pan and cook until brown on all sides, about 3 minutes per side.

4 Pour the wine over the meat and cook until the wine is absorbed, about 5 minutes. Add the tomatoes, stirring well, and reduce the heat to low. Cook slowly until the sauce is creamy, 20 to 25 minutes.

5 Bring a large pot of salted water to a boil. Add the orecchiette and cook until al dente, about 8 minutes. Drain the pasta and transfer it to a bowl. Add the meat's cooking sauce and stir well.

6 Serve the orecchiette with the meat alongside.

VINO To accompany this hearty pasta-and-meat meal, I suggest Nero, a red wine from the Apulia region named for its dark, dense qualities. (*Nero* means "black.")

1½ POUNDS BEEF FROM THE TOP ROUND, CUT BY THE BUTCHER INTO 4 SLICES ABOUT ¼ INCH THICK

FOUR 1-OUNCE ¼-INCH-THICK SLICES PANCETTA

FOUR 1-OUNCE ¼-INCH-THICK SLICES PECORINO TOSCANO

2 TABLESPOONS COARSELY CHOPPED FRESH FLAT-LEAF PARSLEY

1 TABLESPOON COARSELY CHOPPED GARLIC

FINE SEA SALT

FRESHLY GROUND BLACK PEPPER

⅓ CUP EXTRA VIRGIN OLIVE OIL

1 ONION, CHOPPED

1 CUP CHIANTI

1 POUND RIPE ROMA OR PLUM TOMATOES, CUT INTO 8 PIECES EACH AND PASSED THROUGH A FOOD MILL OR GROUND IN A FOOD PROCESSOR WITH THE METAL BLADE

1 POUND ORECCHIETTE

SPEZZATINO DI VITELLO IN GREMOLATA
VEAL STEW WITH GREMOLATA

———

SERVES 4 TO 6 AS A MAIN COURSE

IL CLASSICO

Gremolata, a minced combination of parsley and lemon zest, is the traditional garnish for osso buco.

LA MIA VERSIONE

Here gremolata enlivens a rich stew. To enhance its flavor, this recipe adds orange and rosemary to the mix and instructs you to stir gremolata into the stew for optimum effect. If you can't find veal shoulder, substitute shanks. This dish is delicious with polenta or mashed potatoes.

---

3 TABLESPOONS UNSALTED BUTTER

⅓ CUP EXTRA VIRGIN OLIVE OIL

½ CUP FINELY DICED CELERY

½ CUP FINELY DICED CARROT

1 CUP FINELY DICED ONION

2 POUNDS BONELESS VEAL SHOULDER, TRIMMED AND CUT INTO 1½-INCH CUBES

2 CUPS DRY WHITE WINE

FINE SEA SALT

FRESHLY GROUND BLACK PEPPER

2 LARGE VINE-RIPENED TOMATOES, PEELED, SEEDED, AND CHOPPED (SEE NOTE, PAGE 25)

1 QUART CHICKEN STOCK, SIMMERING IN A SMALL POT ON A BACK BURNER

12 CIPOLLINE OR 30 PEARL ONIONS, PEELED

2 CUPS SMALL WHITE BUTTON MUSHROOMS, CLEANED, STEMS REMOVED

2 FRESH ROSEMARY SPRIGS, FINELY CHOPPED

4 GARLIC CLOVES, FINELY CHOPPED

GRATED ZEST OF 2 ORANGES

GRATED ZEST OF 4 LEMONS

1 Place the butter in a wide heavy flameproof casserole over medium-low heat and add half the olive oil. When the butter has melted, add the celery, carrot, and onion and sauté until golden, stirring occasionally, about 5 minutes.

2 Pour the rest of the olive oil into a skillet over medium-high heat. Add the meat, a little bit at a time, in a single layer. Sear the pieces until brown on all sides, about 4 minutes per side.

3 Add the meat to the casserole with the vegetables, stirring well. Add the wine and season to taste with salt and pepper. When the wine evaporates, after about 5 minutes, add the tomatoes and chicken stock, then cover and simmer for 45 minutes; check occasionally, adding more stock or water if the mixture begins to stick to the bottom of the pan.

4 Add the cipolline and mushrooms and continue to cook until the meat is tender when pricked with a knife, about 10 more minutes.

5 Place the rosemary in a small bowl and add the garlic, orange zest, and lemon zest. Stir well, then add it to the meat when the stew has been removed from the heat. Divide among 4 to 6 plates and serve hot.

VINO The lemon accent of this dish calls for a young Traminer, the distinctive white wine from Friuli.

OSSO BUCO WITH CANNELLINI BEANS

———

SERVES 6 AS A MAIN COURSE

IL CLASSICO

In a country where every major town has its own world-famous specialty, osso buco—veal shank braised in a stew of wine, tomato, onion, and other ingredients—belongs to Milan, where it is served atop saffron-rich risotto alla Milanese and garnished with a pinch of gremolata (roughly chopped parsley and lemon zest). The name of the dish means "bone with a hole," and it is often served with a long spoon for mining the richly flavored marrow.

LA MIA VERSIONE

Although risotto alla Milanese is the historical accompaniment to osso buco, it is far from the only one. Osso buco is best served with something starchy that will soak up its delicious juices; cannellini beans do just that, and the sage adds depth to this sauce.

SIX ¾- TO 1-POUND VEAL SHANKS, CENTER CUT, 2 INCHES THICK

ALL-PURPOSE FLOUR FOR DUSTING THE SHANKS

1½ CUPS EXTRA VIRGIN OLIVE OIL

2 CARROTS, FINELY DICED

2 CELERY RIBS, FINELY DICED

2 ONIONS, FINELY DICED

FINE SEA SALT

FRESHLY GROUND BLACK PEPPER

2 CUPS DRY WHITE WINE

1 CUP TOMATO SAUCE (SEE STEPS 1–3, PAGE 58)

6 CUPS VEAL OR CHICKEN STOCK

¼ POUND DRY PORCINI, SOAKED IN JUST ENOUGH HOT WATER TO COVER BY 1 INCH FOR 20 MINUTES, STRAINED (JUICE STRAINED THROUGH CHEESECLOTH AND RESERVED), AND ROUGHLY CHOPPED

1 HERB SACHET: 1 FRESH ROSEMARY SPRIG, 1 FRESH SAGE LEAF, 1 GARLIC CLOVE, 1 BAY LEAF, TIED IN A CHEESECLOTH BUNDLE

3 CUPS DRIED CANNELLINI BEANS, SOAKED OVERNIGHT IN ENOUGH COLD WATER TO COVER

10 FRESH SAGE LEAVES

4 GARLIC CLOVES

1 Preheat the oven to 375°F.

2 Tie the shanks with kitchen string to keep the meat on the bone during cooking, then dust them with flour.

3 Warm 1 cup of the olive oil in a sauté pan over high heat. Add the shanks and cook until browned on all sides.

4 Coat the bottom of a flameproof casserole with ¼ cup of the remaining olive oil and set over medium heat. Add the carrots, celery, and onions and sweat them until the onion is translucent, about 3 minutes.

5 Add the browned shanks to the casserole with the vegetables. Season with salt and pepper, then drizzle the wine into the casserole. When the wine evaporates, after about 10 minutes, add the tomato sauce. When the tomato sauce has been partially absorbed by the vegetables and meat, after about 5 minutes, add the veal stock, porcini, reserved porcini soaking liquid, and herb sachet. The shanks should be almost covered with liquid; if not, add water to the casserole.

6 Bring to a boil, seal with aluminum foil, and bake until tender, about 1 hour.

7 Remove the foil and cook for 30 minutes more. If the sauce is too thin when the shanks are ready (they should be cooked through but still firm), remove them from the sauce and reduce the sauce until thickened and flavorful.

8 Meanwhile, drain the cannellini beans and transfer them to a pot. Fill the pot with water and add the sage and garlic. Season lightly with salt, bring the liquid to a boil, then reduce the heat to low and simmer very slowly for 40 to 45 minutes, occasionally removing any foam or impurities that rise to the surface, until the beans are cooked but still firm. (If the beans seem soft after soaking, cook them in a wider pot; they will cook more quickly if spread out.)

9 Drain the beans over a bowl and reserve the cooking liquid. Transfer the beans to a

bowl and add a few tablespoons of cooking liquid, the remaining ¼ cup olive oil, and salt and pepper to taste.

10 Serve each shank in the center of a plate, snipping off the kitchen string. Spoon some cannellini all around it. Spoon plenty of sauce on the osso buco and set out a small spoon for the marrow.

VINO Cannellini beans and sage put me in mind of fall, so I recommend a recent-vintage Dolcetto from Piemonte with the osso buco.

VEAL SCALOPPINE WITH EGGPLANT, TOMATO, AND FONTINA

———

SERVES 6 AS A MAIN COURSE

IL CLASSICO

Some of the most popular of all Italian dishes are those made with veal scaloppine. *Scaloppine* refers to a thin, pounded piece of meat, usually sautéed with any of a wide variety of ingredients. When you buy veal scaloppine, be sure the butcher pounds it to an even thickness so that the entire piece cooks at the same rate. Be sure also to get the right cut of veal: a solid piece of meat cut from the top round.

LA MIA VERSIONE

This recipe combines two favorite parmigiana subjects: eggplant and veal.

EGGPLANT

18 EGGPLANT SLICES, SLICED LENGTHWISE ¼ INCH THICK FROM 1 LARGE EGGPLANT

⅔ CUP EXTRA VIRGIN OLIVE OIL

FINE SEA SALT

FRESHLY GROUND BLACK PEPPER

½ CUP CHOPPED FRESH FLAT-LEAF PARSLEY

½ CUP CHOPPED FRESH BASIL

2 GARLIC CLOVES, MINCED

1 Lightly brush both sides of the eggplant with the olive oil and season with salt and pepper.

2 Mix together the parsley, basil, and garlic and spread a little of the mixture on both sides of each eggplant slice. Place on a platter, stacking them if necessary, and marinate for about 2 hours.

3 Cook the eggplant slices on a griddle over medium heat for about 7 minutes, until golden brown on both sides; drizzle the eggplant with any remaining marinade. Set aside.

TOMATOES

1 Preheat the oven to 250°F.

2 Arrange the tomato slices in a single layer on a jelly-roll pan.

3 In a small bowl, stir together the salt and sugar and sprinkle evenly over the tomatoes. Top the tomatoes with the basil, oregano, and garlic and bake for 1 hour or until dry but not shriveled. Raise the oven temperature to 350°F.

EIGHTEEN ½-INCH-THICK SLICES VINE-RIPENED TOMATOES, FROM 4 TO 6 TOMATOES

2 TABLESPOONS FINE SEA SALT

2 TEASPOONS SUGAR

10 FRESH BASIL LEAVES, TORN BY HAND

2 TEASPOONS DRIED OREGANO

3 GARLIC CLOVES, THINLY SLICED

SCALOPPINE AND ASSEMBLY

1 Melt the butter with the olive oil in a sauté pan wide enough to hold the scaloppine in a single layer over medium-high heat.

2 Dredge the scaloppine in flour, shaking off the excess, and place in the pan. Sauté for 2 minutes on each side. You will have to do this in batches. Add a tablespoon or two of the wine to the pan with each batch and cook until evaporated, a few seconds. Season with salt and pepper and remove the veal from the pan, reserving any juice from the pan.

3 Arrange the scaloppine on a baking dish and top them with alternating layers of eggplant, tomatoes, and mozzarella. Bake until the cheese is melted, about 4 minutes. Meanwhile, reheat the cooking juices. Transfer the scaloppine to a serving platter and pour the hot cooking juices over the top. Serve at once.

VINO Serve this with a full-bodied Merlot from Washington State.

2 TABLESPOONS UNSALTED BUTTER

¼ CUP EXTRA VIRGIN OLIVE OIL

18 VEAL SCALOPPINE, ABOUT 2 OUNCES EACH

½ CUP ALL-PURPOSE FLOUR FOR DUSTING

½ CUP DRY WHITE WINE

FINE SEA SALT

FRESHLY GROUND BLACK PEPPER

EIGHTEEN ⅛-INCH-THICK SLICES MOZZARELLA

VIN SANTO POT ROAST WITH CHESTNUT POLENTA AND RAISINS

SERVES 4 AS A MAIN COURSE

IL CLASSICO

Stracotto, which means "long cooked," is an Italian pot roast usually made with an eye of round cooked in red wine.

LA MIA VERSIONE

This recipe brings dessert wine to a stracotto using Vin Santo, which is forceful enough to make an impact even with red meat. The chestnut polenta is a new take on a classic dish that uses chestnut flour rather than cornmeal. If you can't find chestnut flour, make a "regular" polenta.

2 POUNDS BONELESS BEEF SHOULDER OR EYE OF ROUND

3 GARLIC CLOVES, CUT INTO THIN SLIVERS

2 TABLESPOONS UNSALTED BUTTER

2 TABLESPOONS EXTRA VIRGIN OLIVE OIL

3 CUPS VIN SANTO (SEE IN SEARCH OF . . . , PAGE 205)

½ CUP CHOPPED CELERY

¾ CUP CHOPPED CARROT

1½ CUPS CHOPPED ONION

2 TEASPOONS GROUND CINNAMON

1 TEASPOON FRESHLY GRATED NUTMEG

4 CLOVES

5 CUPS VEAL OR CHICKEN STOCK, SIMMERING IN A POT ON A BACK BURNER

FINE SEA SALT

FRESHLY GROUND BLACK PEPPER

2 CUPS CIPOLLINE OR PEARL ONIONS, PEELED

2 CUPS WHOLE MILK

1 FRESH ROSEMARY SPRIG

1 TABLESPOON SUGAR

2 CUPS CHESTNUT FLOUR OR YELLOW CORNMEAL

⅓ CUP RAISINS, SOAKED IN WATER FOR AT LEAST 5 MINUTES

1 Tie the meat crosswise with kitchen string at 1-inch intervals. Use a sharp, thin-bladed knife to cut slits in the beef and slide a garlic sliver into each slit.

2 Melt the butter with the olive oil in a pot over medium-high heat, then add the meat and cook until brown on all sides, about 5 minutes per side.

3 Add the Vin Santo and cook until reduced by half, about 10 minutes. Add the celery, carrot, onion, cinnamon, nutmeg, cloves, and stock and season to taste with salt and pepper. Cover, lower the heat, and cook at a gentle simmer for 2 hours; when the meat is almost cooked (after about 1 hour and 45 minutes), add the cipolline.

4 Meanwhile, make the polenta: pour the milk into a pot over medium heat. Add 1 quart water and the rosemary and sugar and season with salt. Bring the liquid to a boil.

5 Fill another small pot with water and bring it to a boil.

6 Add the chestnut flour to the milk-water mixture, mixing continuously with a whisk to avoid lumps; if the polenta gets too thick, add some boiling water from the other pot so the polenta has a creamy consistency. Cook over very low heat for 6 to 7 minutes; then taste, adjust the seasoning, and set aside, covered, to keep the polenta warm, or keep it warm in the top of a double boiler over simmering water.

7 Remove the meat and cipolline from the pan and pass the sauce through a fine-mesh strainer. Return the sauce to the pan and cook over low heat, reducing it until it is creamy.

8 Drain the raisins and add them to the sauce.

9 To serve, slice the meat, add the cipolline to the sauce, and spoon the sauce over the meat. Serve the polenta on the side.

VINO An intensely flavored dish like this calls for a great bottle of reserve Barolo from Piemonte.

LAMB SHANK WITH CAULIFLOWER AND RED PEPPER

———

SERVES 4 AS A MAIN COURSE

IL CLASSICO

The shank is considered by some to be one of the tastiest cuts there is. The meat derives a lot of flavor from being located so close to the bone, and it becomes super-tender when slow-cooked. Most shank recipes reheat well, so even though they require long, slow cooking, they can be made ahead of time. Lamb shanks cut from the shoulder end are meatier than those from the hind legs.

LA MIA VERSIONE

While lamb shank is a classic winter dish, often served with white bean stew, this is a decidedly lighter version with cauliflower and red pepper. Serve this with soft polenta.

4 LAMB SHANKS

⅓ CUP ALL-PURPOSE FLOUR

⅓ CUP EXTRA VIRGIN OLIVE OIL

4 TABLESPOONS (½ STICK) UNSALTED BUTTER

1 CELERY RIB, CHOPPED

1 CARROT, CHOPPED

1 ONION, CHOPPED

FINE SEA SALT

FRESHLY GROUND BLACK PEPPER

2 CUPS CHIANTI

5 CUPS VEGETABLE STOCK, PLUS MORE IF NEEDED

1 HERB SACHET: 3 FRESH THYME SPRIGS, 1 BAY LEAF, 2 GARLIC CLOVES, 1 TEASPOON BLACK PEPPERCORNS, 2 CLOVES, 1 TEASPOON JUNIPER BERRIES, TIED IN A CHEESECLOTH BUNDLE

1 RED ONION, HALVED AND THINLY SLICED

2 YELLOW BELL PEPPERS, CUT INTO 1-INCH STRIPS

2 RED BELL PEPPERS, CUT INTO 1-INCH STRIPS

1 HEAD CAULIFLOWER (ABOUT 1 POUND), FLORETS ONLY

(continued)

1 Preheat the oven to 350°F.

2 Dredge the lamb shanks in flour. Warm a third of the olive oil in a skillet and brown the shanks on all sides.

3 In another ovenproof pan, melt the butter with another third of the olive oil over medium-low heat. Add the celery, carrot, and onion and sauté for about 20 minutes over medium-low heat. Add the shanks and season with salt and pepper. Pour the wine over the meat and cook until evaporated, about 10 minutes. Add the vegetable stock and the herb sachet. Cover and braise in the oven for about 1½ hours. Check periodically to make sure the sauce covers the meat at all times (add some vegetable stock if necessary).

4 Meanwhile, heat the rest of the olive oil in a skillet. Add the red onion and sauté until translucent, about 4 minutes. Add the bell peppers, season with salt, and cook over medium heat for 5 minutes. Remove from the heat and cover to keep warm.

5 After the shanks have been cooking for 1½ hours, add the cauliflower and sautéed peppers and onions to the pot, stir well, and return to the oven, uncovered, for 15 more minutes. Place 1 shank on each of 4 dinner plates, top with some sauce and vegetables, and serve.

VINO This lamb dish demands a great reserve Brunello di Montalcino.

LEG OF LAMB WITH GORGONZOLA SPREAD

SERVES 6 TO 8 AS A MAIN COURSE

IL CLASSICO

Whole roasted leg of lamb is an Italian favorite, usually enlivened with a paste of garlic and herbs that's rubbed into the meat before cooking.

LA MIA VERSIONE

This recipe turns whole roasted leg of lamb into a decadent affair with a spread of Gorgonzola that melts into the meat when cooked. This is delicious with roasted potatoes and/or a mâche salad tossed with a teaspoon or two of olive oil and genuine balsamic vinegar, aceto balsamico tradizionale di Modena (page 191).

1 Preheat the oven to 325°F.

2 Use a sharp, thin-bladed knife to cut slits in the meat and slide a garlic sliver into each slit. Season all over with salt and pepper (being mindful of the fact that the Gorgonzola is salty), then spread the cheese all over the leg of lamb. Sprinkle the rosemary and thyme leaves on it, then wrap the leg in caul fat.

3 Place the leg in a roasting pan and roast for 30 minutes. Pour the white wine over the leg and roast for about 30 minutes more for medium-rare. (An instant-read thermometer inserted to the center of the leg should read 130°F.) Remove from the oven and let rest for 10 minutes.

4 Remove the caul fat, carve the leg, and serve at once.

VINO Savor this with a full-bodied reserve Brunello di Montalcino.

- **1 LEG OF LAMB, ABOUT 5 POUNDS, RINSED AND TRIMMED OF FAT**
- **3 GARLIC CLOVES, CUT INTO THIN SLIVERS**
- **FINE SEA SALT**
- **FRESHLY GROUND BLACK PEPPER**
- **¾ POUND CREAMY GORGONZOLA AT ROOM TEMPERATURE**
- **LEAVES FROM 2 FRESH ROSEMARY SPRIGS**
- **LEAVES FROM 2 FRESH THYME SPRIGS**
- **1 POUND CAUL FAT, SOAKED IN COOL WATER FOR AT LEAST 30 MINUTES**
- **2 CUPS DRY WHITE WINE**

VEAL CHOP WITH CHICKEN LIVER SAUCE

SERVES 4 AS A MAIN COURSE

IL CLASSICO

This recipe was inspired by lombatina finanziera, a northern Italian dish consisting of a broiled veal chop served in a brown butter sauce with chicken liver and capers.

LA MIA VERSIONE

The sauce here is granted added complexity by the chopped salami and anchovy. Serve this with sautéed broccoli rabe or a simple fresh fennel salad tossed with olive oil, salt, and pepper.

½ CUP PLUS 3 TABLESPOONS EXTRA VIRGIN OLIVE OIL

FOUR 1-INCH-THICK VEAL CHOPS

FINE SEA SALT

FRESHLY GROUND BLACK PEPPER

3 ANCHOVY FILLETS

2 SLICES TUSCAN FINOCCHIONA (A TYPE OF SALAMI) OR ITALIAN SALAMI

2 GARLIC CLOVES

¼ POUND CHICKEN LIVERS

JUICE AND ZEST OF 1 LEMON

1 TABLESPOON CHOPPED FRESH FLAT-LEAF PARSLEY

2 TABLESPOONS WHITE WINE VINEGAR

1 Warm 3 tablespoons of the olive oil in a sauté pan wide enough to hold the chops over medium-high heat. Add the chops and brown them for 2 minutes on each side, seasoning with salt and pepper when turning them. When the chops are golden brown, lower the heat to low and cook for 4 to 5 minutes more on each side. Transfer the chops to a warm dish and cover to keep them warm.

2 Place the anchovies, salami, 1 garlic clove, and the chicken livers on a cutting board and chop them together to form a paste. Transfer to a bowl and add the lemon zest and parsley. Stir to form a homogenous mixture.

3 Heat the remaining ½ cup olive oil in a small flameproof casserole and brown the remaining garlic clove, then remove and discard it. Stir in the chicken liver mixture and drizzle it with the lemon juice and vinegar. Cook for 5 to 6 minutes.

4 Serve the chops from a platter or individual plates, topped with the sauce.

VINO This strongly flavored dish requires a full-bodied Cabernet from California.

COSTOLETTE D'AGNELLO ALLA GRIGLIA IN MARINATA DI LIMONE

LEMON-MARINATED LAMB CHOPS

SERVES 6 AS A MAIN COURSE

IL CLASSICO

This recipe is based on the lemon and oregano marinade that Marta, my corporate chef, learned from her grandmother and that was used to marinate everything from lamb to goat.

LA MIA VERSIONE

The acidic marinade goes wonderfully with the sweetness of roasted peppers. If you're not adept at frenching lamb chops (trimming the bone end), ask your butcher to do it for you; it makes a beautiful presentation. If you like, serve this with a small green salad tossed with olive oil and vinegar.

1 Coarsely chop the onion, garlic, and lemon zest and place in a stand mixer or food processor with the metal blade with the wine, dried and fresh oregano, and ¾ cup of the olive oil. Season with salt and pepper and process until a coarse mixture is formed.

2 Rub the chops with this marinade, then place them in the refrigerator, covered, for at least 2 hours or overnight. Do not remove from the marinade until just before grilling.

3 Roast the peppers over the flame of a gas burner, turning them frequently with the help of a long fork or tongs to roast them evenly on all sides. (You can also do this under the broiler.) Place them in a bowl sealed with plastic wrap for ½ hour; then peel them, removing all the burned skin; to make this easier, you can peel the peppers under running water. Cut the peppers into 1-inch-wide strips.

4 If you're using the grapes, press them in a potato ricer or a food mill and transfer the juice to a small casserole. Cook over low heat to reduce it by half, then remove from the heat and let cool. Skip this step if you're using verjus.

5 Place 1 teaspoon salt in a small bowl. Add the cooled grape liquid or verjus and stir to dissolve the salt. Add the remaining 6 tablespoons olive oil in a thin stream, whisking to emulsify. Add the peppers, anchovies, chopped red onion, and parsley. Cover and marinate for 3 hours.

(continued)

1 SMALL ONION

1 GARLIC CLOVE

GRATED ZEST OF 1 LEMON

1 TABLESPOON DRY WHITE WINE

1 TEASPOON DRIED OREGANO

1 TABLESPOON FRESH OREGANO LEAVES

1 CUP PLUS 2 TABLESPOONS EXTRA VIRGIN OLIVE OIL

FINE SEA SALT

FRESHLY GROUND BLACK PEPPER

12 LAMB CHOPS, FRENCHED AND TRIMMED

2 YELLOW BELL PEPPERS

2 RED BELL PEPPERS

1 POUND WHITE GRAPES OR 3 TABLESPOONS VERJUS

4 ANCHOVY FILLETS, ROUGHLY CHOPPED

1 RED ONION, CHOPPED

2 TABLESPOONS CHOPPED FRESH FLAT-LEAF PARSLEY

6 Prepare an outdoor grill for grilling.

7 Grill the chops to desired doneness. Season with salt and freshly ground black pepper. Serve at once, topped with the roasted pepper dressing.

VINO A young Pinot Noir from Washington State will complement the delicate lamb.

CHEESE AND DESSERT

For most children, the idea of having their mouth cleaned out is a frightful experience carried out by a disapproving father armed with a bar of soap. But when my father taught me to clean my mouth out, it was a very positive experience, carried out at the end of a meal, with cheese, dessert, or a combination of the two.

My father had a strong conviction that it was essential to punctuate a meal at its end and that this was to be done not with an overstated exclamation point but with a confident little period. You ended a meal by tastefully and humbly cleansing your mouth with one final lingering sensation, a sweet veil of pleasure that would bottle up the experience of the meal and allow you to get on your way, fully satisfied but not suffering the aftershock of overindulgence.

We did not enjoy big, elaborate desserts after a meal in my home. To us cheese was an alternative to dessert or dessert was something as simple as a great fruit gelato, which is an art form all its own. To this day, I am not sure which I had first, a ripe piece of fruit or a great fruit gelato, because our gelati so captured the essence of fruit that in memory they are indistinguishable. Or whether my first experience of caciotta was enjoyed with a slice of pear after lunch or with cold cuts beforehand. Did I first enjoy fresh ricotta spread on toast before dinner or after dinner in a cheesecake? I don't know.

In this chapter I share some of my favorite cheese and fruit combinations and a few cheese and vegetable combinations as well.

The desserts featured here offer a quick, sweet little tour of Italy, with selections not just from Tuscany but also from Naples, Sicily, and Rome. Some are based on desserts you might purchase from a street cart, and others are based on lost and long-forgotten recipes that we've rediscovered and made new again.

These recipes are not elaborate. They are straightforward, and I think they represent how people like to eat. They are as unconventional in concept as they are humble in execution. I think they are a fine way to end a meal or enjoy the taste of something sweet at any time of day.

PIATTO D'INVERNO

WINTER CHEESE PLATE

SERVES 6 TO 8 AS A CHEESE COURSE

IL CLASSICO

Without question the most-well-known Italian blue cheese is Gorgonzola. There are two types of Gorgonzola: dolce, or sweet, which is the type most people are familiar with, and naturale, an aged variety.

LA MIA VERSIONE

Rather than accompanying the Gorgonzola with different families of cheeses, this cheese course introduces Gorgonzola to its Spanish and British counterparts: Cabrales and Stilton, the most famous blues in their respective nations. Because blue cheese is so assertive, it is paired here with sweet accompaniments to cut through the rich flavor.

1 POUND GORGONZOLA DI NOVARA

1 POUND CABRALES

1 POUND STILTON

1 SLICE (ABOUT ½ POUND) QUINCE PASTE

16 DATES

16 DRIED FIGS

1 LOAF WARM WALNUT BREAD

Arrange the Gorgonzola, Cabrales, and Stilton on a nonreactive tray and artfully adorn the tray with the quince paste, dates, and dried figs. Serve with warm walnut bread.

VINO Serve this with a slightly fruity sweet wine like Sauternes.

TUSCAN CHEESE PLATE

SERVES 6 TO 8 AS A CHEESE COURSE

IL CLASSICO

Without a doubt the most acclaimed Pecorino in Italy is Pecorino Toscano, the young sheep's-milk cheese served with fava beans every spring . . .

LA MIA VERSIONE

. . . but there are other Pecorinos also worth discovering. This cheese plate matches Pecorino Toscano with less-well-known Pecorinos: Rossellino, which is aged for six months and rubbed with tomato paste, and a Stravecchio, a longer-aged Pecorino that comes wrapped in walnut leaves. Because all of these cheeses are rather dense, they are accompanied by sweet counterparts like apple, pear, and honey.

1 POUND FRESH PECORINO TOSCANO

1 POUND PECORINO ROSSELLINO (FROM PIENZA)

1 POUND PECORINO STRAVECCHIO (WRAPPED IN WALNUT LEAVES)

2 RIPE PEARS

2 GRANNY SMITH APPLES

JUICE OF 1 LEMON

ROSEMARY HONEY

CHESTNUT HONEY

1 LOAF TUSCAN COUNTRY BREAD, SLICED AND WARMED

1 Arrange the Pecorino Toscano, Rossellino, and Stravecchio on a nonreactive tray.

2 Rinse and slice the pears and apples, leaving the skin on, and rub them with lemon juice to keep them from discoloring. Pat them dry with a towel and place on the tray.

3 Serve with the honey alongside, encouraging your guests to enjoy the rosemary honey with the fresh Pecorino Toscano and Rossellino and the chestnut honey with the Stravecchio. Serve the bread alongside.

VINO Serve this with a full-bodied red like Dolcetto.

NORTHERN CHEESE PLATE

———

SERVES 6 TO 8 AS A CHEESE COURSE

IL CLASSICO

Mostarda di Cremona is a sweet-and-sour fruit condiment from northern Italy traditionally served with various meats.

LA MIA VERSIONE

Here this fruit mustard is paired instead with assertive cheese.

1½ POUNDS STRACCHINO OR CRESCENZA, SOFTENED FOR A FEW HOURS AT ROOM TEMPERATURE

ONE 1-POUND JAR MOSTARDA DI CREMONA (AVAILABLE FROM ITALIAN SPECIALTY STORES)

1 LOAF ITALIAN WHITE BREAD, SLICED AND TOASTED

Place the cheese on a serving platter and the mostarda in a bowl. Taste them together with a slice of bread.

VINO Serve this with a full-bodied California Chardonnay.

EMILIA-ROMAGNA CHEESE PLATE

SERVES 6 TO 8 AS A CHEESE COURSE

IL CLASSICO

Parmigiano-Reggiano and balsamic vinegar are two of the most famous products of the Parma area.

LA MIA VERSIONE

This plate puts these two treasures together. Not surprisingly, they get along brilliantly.

1½ POUNDS PARMIGIANO-REGGIANO, AGED ABOUT 2 YEARS

4 RIPE PEARS, RINSED, CORED, QUARTERED, AND RUBBED WITH LEMON JUICE

1 POUND RED GRAPES, RINSED AND DRIED

ACETO BALSAMICO TRADIZIONALE DI MODENA (SEE IN SEARCH OF . . . , PAGE 191)

1 LOAF WALNUT-RAISIN BREAD, WARMED

1 Place the Parmigiano on a wooden cutting board and the pears and grapes in a bowl.

2 Use a small knife to break the Parmigiano into small chunks and top with a few drops of balsamic vinegar. Serve with the walnut-raisin bread alongside.

VINO The complex vinegar calls for a big wine that won't be overwhelmed by it. Select a California Cabernet Sauvignon.

ROMAN CHEESE PLATE

SERVES 6 AS A CHEESE COURSE

IL CLASSICO

Bocconcini (mouthfuls) are small balls of fresh mozzarella, traditionally enjoyed as part of an antipasto selection. Authentic mozzarella from outside Naples is made with water buffalo milk (mozzarella di bufala). It is often available at gourmet shops.

LA MIA VERSIONE

In this recipe the bocconcini are made part of a salad. Serve this as an unusual cheese course after a particularly rich dinner.

FINE SEA SALT

3 TABLESPOONS FRESH LEMON JUICE

¼ CUP PLUS 1 TABLESPOON EXTRA VIRGIN OLIVE OIL

6 BUNCHES BABY ARUGULA, RINSED AND SPUN DRY

FRESHLY GROUND BLACK PEPPER

4 MOZZARELLA DI BUFALA BOCCONCINI, 3 TO 4 OUNCES EACH

1 LOAF WHOLE WHEAT BREAD, SLICED AND TOASTED

1 In a small bowl, use a whisk to dissolve ¼ teaspoon salt into the lemon juice, then add the olive oil and whisk until emulsified.

2 Place the arugula in a bowl and toss it with the dressing, mixing thoroughly. Season with pepper.

3 Slice the mozzarella and place it on a serving platter with the arugula salad. Serve the warm toasted bread alongside.

VINO Serve this with a young Frascati from the Lazio region.

SALTED FOCACCIA WITH FRESH RICOTTA AND CHOCOLATE

SERVES 8 TO 10

IL CLASSICO

In the old part of Rome, there is a bakery where I used to stand on line every morning so I could begin my day with my favorite all-time breakfast: a square foot of focaccia sprinkled with rock sea salt and spread with Nutella.

LA MIA VERSIONE

This richer version adds creamy ricotta, bridging the salt and chocolate.

2 OUNCES FRESH YEAST

2 TABLESPOONS SUGAR

3 TABLESPOONS EXTRA VIRGIN OLIVE OIL

1 TABLESPOON FINE SEA SALT

2½ POUNDS ALL-PURPOSE FLOUR, PLUS MORE FOR DUSTING THE WORK SURFACE

1 POUND FRESH SHEEP'S-MILK RICOTTA

1 JAR CHOCOLATE SPREAD OR NUTELLA

1 Place 1¾ cups warm water, the yeast, sugar, and olive oil in a bowl (or in the bowl of a mixer fitted with the plastic paddle) and mix with a wooden spoon (or the electric mixer paddle). Then let sit until bubbles form, about 10 minutes. Add the salt and flour and mix, using the dough hook of an electric mixer, for about 10 minutes, or by hand until all the liquid is absorbed. Turn the mixture out onto a floured work surface and knead the dough until smooth and elastic.

2 Oil a jelly-roll pan and use your hands to distribute the dough evenly. Let proof at room temperature, keeping it out of any drafts, for about 2 hours.

3 Preheat the oven to 400°F.

4 When the dough has doubled in bulk, place the pan in the oven and bake until the focaccia is golden and crispy on top and cooked in the center (a toothpick inserted in the middle should come out clean), 20 to 25 minutes.

5 Remove the pan from the oven and let cool until warm. Turn out the focaccia, cut it in half horizontally, and spread one side with the ricotta and the other with the chocolate. Place the halves together and cut into small sandwiches.

RADICCHIO TREVIGIANO AND TALEGGIO

SERVES 4 AS A CHEESE COURSE

IL CLASSICO

Taleggio is a raw cow's-milk cheese from northern Italy that is traditionally served with bread and wine or thinly sliced and melted over polenta. You may need to seek it out from a specialty store, because it is produced in very small batches.

LA MIA VERSIONE

The buttery flavor of Taleggio is a perfect foil for bitter radicchio. Here the two are baked together for a simple but memorable duet.

4 HEADS RADICCHIO TREVIGIANO, ROOT TRIMMED AND HEADS CUT IN HALF LENGTHWISE

FINE SEA SALT

FRESHLY GROUND BLACK PEPPER

¼ CUP EXTRA VIRGIN OLIVE OIL

1 POUND TALEGGIO, CRUST REMOVED AND SLICED ¼ INCH THICK

1 CUP TOASTED WALNUT HALVES, COARSELY CHOPPED

1 Preheat the oven to 350°F.

2 Arrange the radicchio, cut side up, on a cookie sheet, season with salt and pepper, and drizzle with half the olive oil.

3 Top with the Taleggio slices and bake for 15 minutes. Remove from the oven and heat the broiler. Place the cookie sheet under the broiler for 2 to 3 minutes to brown the cheese lightly. Divide the radicchio among individual plates, sprinkle with the walnuts, and serve.

VINO Serve this with a chilled Barbera, a red wine from Emilia-Romagna.

EGGPLANT-CHOCOLATE MOUSSE

SERVES 8

IL CLASSICO

This dessert was popular among the Neapolitan aristocracy in the 1800s, created by chefs as a rebellion to formal French pastry. Essentially it "Napolitizes" a chocolate mousse by combining it with caramelized eggplant that will pleasantly surprise you with its sweet softness.

LA MIA VERSIONE

Marta, my corporate chef, rediscovered this recipe while we were preparing to open Centolire. This is one of those dishes that is presented in this book as it was originally cooked, but will seem brand-new to anyone to whom you serve it.

1 Preheat the oven to 400°F.

2 Separate the whole eggs and place the 2 yolks in a mixing bowl. Add 2 tablespoons of the granulated sugar and beat well. Add the flour, 1 tablespoon of the cocoa powder, and the baking powder, then fold in the 2 egg whites.

3 Line 2 sheet pans with parchment paper, spray them with nonstick spray, and spread the mixture on one of the pans to a thickness of 1 inch. Bake for 7 to 10 minutes, until golden on top.

4 Remove the sponge cake from the oven, turn it upside down, and cover it with a damp clean towel.

5 Place 4 tablespoons of the butter in a nonstick pan over medium heat. When the butter has melted, add the sliced eggplant and cook until browned on both sides, about 4 minutes per side.

6 Add 3 tablespoons raw brown sugar to help caramelize the eggplant slices. When they have caramelized, transfer them to the unused sheet pan.

7 Place the rest of the butter in the nonstick pan. When it has melted, add the diced eggplant and cook until brown, about 5 minutes. Add the remaining raw brown sugar

2 WHOLE LARGE EGGS PLUS 2 LARGE YOLKS

1¼ CUPS PLUS 2 TABLESPOONS GRANULATED SUGAR

1½ TABLESPOONS ALL-PURPOSE FLOUR, SIFTED

2 TABLESPOONS UNSWEETENED COCOA POWDER

¼ TEASPOON BAKING POWDER

6 TABLESPOONS UNSALTED BUTTER

6 ITALIAN EGGPLANTS, 2 SLICED ⅛ INCH THICK, 4 CUT INTO ¼-INCH DICE

1¼ CUPS RAW BROWN SUGAR (TURBINADO)

1 CUP WHOLE MILK

½ CUP EGG WHITES (FROM ABOUT 3 LARGE EGGS), WHIPPED UNTIL STIFF

1 LEAF GELATIN, SOAKED IN COLD WATER

3½ OUNCES BITTERSWEET CHOCOLATE, CHOPPED

1 CUP HEAVY CREAM, WHIPPED

and cook until caramelized, then remove the diced eggplant from the pan and place on the cookie sheet with the eggplant slices.

8 Place the 2 egg yolks in a mixing bowl, add 3 tablespoons of the remaining granulated sugar, and beat well.

9 Place the milk in a saucepan over high heat and bring it to a boil. Slowly add the hot milk to the egg-sugar mixture. Transfer to the top of a double boiler and cook, whisking continuously, until the cream clings to the spoon.

10 Whip the egg whites with the remaining granulated sugar until stiff peaks form.

11 Squeeze the gelatin to remove as much moisture as possible and add it to the cream. Add the rest of the cocoa and the chopped chocolate. Let the mixture cool, then fold it into the whipped heavy cream, then fold in the egg whites–sugar mixture. Add the caramelized diced eggplant, stirring carefully.

12 Spray a nonstick cake mold with nonstick spray, then line it with the slices of caramelized eggplant and add the chocolate mousse. Cut the sponge cake to the same diameter as the mold and cover the mousse with it.

13 Place in the refrigerator for at least 4 hours or overnight, then carefully turn it upside down onto a serving platter and slice to serve.

TAGLIATELLE TORTA WITH APPLES AND RAISINS

SERVES 8

IL CLASSICO

The tagliatelle torta, a cake made by baking fresh tagliatelle in a pie plate, is a classic dish from the South of Italy. There are many great variations, the most famous one featuring almonds and chocolate.

LA MIA VERSIONE

This is the version we serve at Centolire in New York City, a much lighter rendition than most of the traditional ones.

1¾ CUPS ALL-PURPOSE FLOUR, PLUS MORE FOR DUSTING THE WORK SURFACE

6 TABLESPOONS UNSALTED BUTTER

½ TEASPOON BAKING POWDER

ZEST OF 1 LEMON

3 LARGE EGGS

2 CUPS GRANULATED SUGAR

½ CUP RAISINS

1 CUP WARM BREWED EARL GREY TEA

FINE SEA SALT

½ POUND FRESH TAGLIATELLE

1 LARGE GRANNY SMITH APPLE, PEELED, CORED, AND GRATED

½ CUP CHOPPED ALMONDS

PINCH OF GROUND CINNAMON

1 TABLESPOON CONFECTIONERS' SUGAR

1 Preheat the oven to 350°F.

2 Place the flour in the bowl of a mixer fitted with the plastic paddle. Add the butter, baking powder, lemon zest, one of the eggs, and 1 cup of the granulated sugar. Mix until the ingredients just hold together.

3 Dust a work surface with flour and place the mixture on it. Knead for about 1 minute, just enough to make a ball. Wrap in plastic wrap and refrigerate for at least 30 minutes.

4 Flour a work surface and roll the dough out ⅛ inch thick. Fit inside a 10-inch spring-form pan. (It will come almost all the way up the sides.)

5 Place the raisins in the warm tea and set aside to soak.

6 Pour enough water into a pot to completely immerse the tagliatelle. Add a pinch of salt and bring to a boil over high heat, then add the pasta and cook until al dente, 2 to 3 minutes. Drain the pasta and place it on a cookie sheet to cool.

7 Separate the remaining eggs and place the yolks in a mixing bowl. Add the rest of the granulated sugar and beat well by hand. Drain the raisins and add them to the bowl, then add the apple, almonds, and cinnamon, stirring well.

8 Place the egg whites in another mixing bowl and whip them to stiff peaks. Fold them into the egg yolk mixture, then carefully add the pasta, mixing well.

9 Fill the springform pan with the mixture and bake for about 35 minutes, until set and golden. If the top gets too brown, cover with aluminum foil.

10 Let cool slightly, remove the sides of the pan, dust with the confectioners' sugar, slice into individual portions, and serve.

TORTA DI CREMA E PINOLI

CREAM AND PINE NUT TART

———

SERVES 8 TO 10

IL CLASSICO

Torta della nonna (grandmother's cake) is a very rich cake of pastry cream and nuts that has been popular throughout Italy for centuries.

LA MIA VERSIONE

This is an even richer version than the original, with fresh ricotta cheese and pine nuts added to the traditional formula.

1¼ CUPS ALL-PURPOSE FLOUR, PLUS MORE FOR DUSTING THE WORK SURFACE

2¼ CUPS GRANULATED SUGAR

12 TABLESPOONS (1½ STICKS) UNSALTED BUTTER, PLUS MORE FOR GREASING THE PAN

1 TEASPOON BAKING POWDER

ZEST OF 2 LEMONS, REMOVED IN 1-INCH STRIPS, PLUS 1 TABLESPOON GRATED LEMON ZEST

2 WHOLE LARGE EGGS PLUS 3 LARGE YOLKS

1 TABLESPOON DURUM FLOUR (SEE IN SEARCH OF . . . , PAGE 16) OR ALL-PURPOSE FLOUR

1 TEASPOON CONFECTIONERS' SUGAR, PLUS MORE FOR DUSTING IF DESIRED

2 CUPS HOT WHOLE MILK

1 CUP FRESH RICOTTA, SQUEEZED IN CHEESECLOTH IF WATERY

2 TABLESPOONS COARSELY CHOPPED TOASTED PINE NUTS

FRESH STRAWBERRIES FOR GARNISH (OPTIONAL)

1 Preheat the oven to 375°F.

2 Place the all-purpose flour in the bowl of a mixer fitted with the plastic paddle and add 2 cups of the granulated sugar, the butter, baking powder, lemon zest strips, and whole eggs. Mix until the ingredients just hold together.

3 Dust a work surface with flour and place the dough on it. Knead for about 1 minute, just enough to make a ball. Wrap the dough in plastic wrap and refrigerate for at least 30 minutes.

4 Place the egg yolks in the bowl of an electric mixer, add the remaining granulated sugar, and beat until fluffy, about 5 minutes. Add the durum flour, grated lemon zest, and confectioners' sugar, then reduce the speed and continue to beat while slowly pouring in the hot milk, until amalgamated.

5 Place the mixture in a nonreactive double boiler or bowl placed over simmering water. Cook, mixing continuously with a wooden spoon, until the cream thickens to a spreadable consistency. Remove from the heat and cool to room temperature.

6 Place the ricotta in a mixing bowl and whip it with an electric mixer or a whisk until smooth. Fold in the cream and pine nuts, mixing until well amalgamated.

7 Grease a 10-inch springform pan with butter or vegetable oil. Divide the dough into 2 pieces, one a little bigger than the other. Roll out the bigger ball and line the bot-

tom and sides of the pan with it. Add the ricotta mixture to the mold, stirring, then roll out the smaller ball of dough and cover the mixture with it. Pinch the ends together, pressing with your fingers, to seal the mold. Pierce the top with a fork and cover with aluminum foil. Bake for 40 minutes, then remove the foil and bake for 6 to 7 minutes more, until golden.

8 Remove from the oven, let cool down to warm, then remove the sides of the pan and serve. If desired, dust with confectioners' sugar and serve with fresh strawberries on the side.

RICOTTA AND CANDIED FRUIT SEMIFREDDO

—

SERVES 6

IL CLASSICO

Semifreddo is a semifrozen custard dessert. A cassata is a Sicilian sponge cake filled with ricotta cheese and candied fruits.

LA MIA VERSIONE

This recipe combines the characteristics of a semifreddo and a cassata for a super-refreshing dessert that is both cold and tart.

½ POUND FRESH RICOTTA, SQUEEZED IN CHEESECLOTH IF WATERY

1¼ CUPS HEAVY CREAM

5 TABLESPOONS CONFECTIONERS' SUGAR, SIFTED

¼ CUP BLANCHED ALMONDS, LIGHTLY TOASTED AND COARSELY CHOPPED

¼ CUP PISTACHIOS, COARSELY CHOPPED

ZEST OF 1 LEMON, JULIENNED WITH A ZESTER

ZEST OF 1 ORANGE, JULIENNED WITH A ZESTER

¼ CUP COARSELY CHOPPED SEMISWEET CHOCOLATE

1½ CUPS STRAWBERRIES, RINSED AND PATTED DRY

1 Place the ricotta in a mixing bowl and whip it with an electric mixer or a whisk until smooth.

2 Place the heavy cream in a mixing bowl and whip it while adding the sugar a little at a time, until well incorporated.

3 Fold the whipped cream into the ricotta, then add the following ingredients one at a time, mixing carefully: almonds, pistachios, lemon zest, orange zest, and chocolate.

4 Refrigerate until serving, but don't let it sit for more than an hour, or it will lose its fluffiness. Add the strawberries just before serving so that they don't "bleed out" and color the dish.

BUTTERNUT SQUASH GELATO WITH FALL SPICES

_____

SERVES 6 TO 8

IL CLASSICO

Gelato, the soft Italian ice cream, is usually flavored with fruit, chocolate, coffee, nuts, or other things we associate with dessert.

LA MIA VERSIONE

It turns out that butternut squash is a natural for gelato as well. Its sweet flavor is delicious in this smooth, cool context, especially when enhanced with cardamom, clove, ginger, and nutmeg.

---

2 CUPS HEAVY CREAM

2 CUPS WHOLE MILK

1¼ CUPS RAW BROWN SUGAR (TURBINADO)

¼ TEASPOON FINE SEA SALT

4 LARGE EGG YOLKS

2 CUPS HOMEMADE OR CANNED BUTTERNUT SQUASH PUREE

¼ TEASPOON GROUND CARDAMOM

1 TEASPOON FRESHLY GRATED NUTMEG

¼ TEASPOON GROUND CLOVES

¼ TEASPOON GROUND GINGER

TOASTED WALNUTS FOR GARNISH (OPTIONAL)

WHIPPED CREAM (OPTIONAL)

1 Pour the cream into a large heavy flameproof casserole and add the milk, brown sugar, and salt. Bring the liquid to a boil over low heat, stirring until the sugar has dissolved.

2 Place the egg yolks in a bowl and beat them with a whisk until they turn pale yellow. Gradually add the milk mixture, whisking continuously.

3 Pour the mixture into the top of a double boiler set over low heat or into a bowl set on top of simmering water. Cook until the mixture coats the back of a spoon, then remove from the heat and let cool.

4 Place the butternut squash puree in a bowl and add 1 cup of the milk mixture, whisking continuously. Add the butternut squash mixture, cardamom, nutmeg, cloves, and ginger to the milk mixture, whisking continuously.

5 Process in an ice cream machine, following the manufacturer's instructions. If desired, serve with some toasted walnuts and/or whipped cream.

CHOCOLATE PUDDING WITH CHERRY SAUCE

SERVES 8 TO 10

IL CLASSICO

Chocolate pudding is a childhood favorite, as much in Italy as it is in America.

LA MIA VERSIONE

This variation on classic pudding adds cherries macerated in wine. The contrast reinforces the semisweet flavor of the chocolate.

CHOCOLATE PUDDING

1 Pour the milk into a pot and add the chopped chocolate. Cut the vanilla bean in half lengthwise; scrape the seeds into the milk, and add the pod to the milk as well. Cook over low heat, stirring frequently, until it reaches a boil. When the chocolate is melted, add the sugar and ladyfingers. Simmer for 30 minutes, stirring frequently with a wooden spoon to keep the mixture from sticking to the bottom of the pan.

2 Remove from the heat and cool to room temperature, then pass the mixture through a fine-mesh strainer set over a bowl. Add the eggs, one at time, whisking with a whisk, to amalgamate all the ingredients.

2 QUARTS WHOLE MILK

4½ OUNCES SEMISWEET CHOCOLATE, FINELY CHOPPED

1 VANILLA BEAN

1 CUP SUGAR

4½ OUNCES LADYFINGERS, CRUMBLED BY HAND

6 LARGE EGGS

CARAMEL

Place the sugar in a sauté pan, add 2 tablespoons water, and cook over low heat until the sugar caramelizes. Don't stir it at any point. Remove from the heat and pour into a 2-quart oven-proof pudding mold to coat.

1 CUP SUGAR

CHERRY SAUCE AND ASSEMBLY

1 Preheat the oven to 350°F.

2 Pour the chocolate mixture into the caramel-coated pudding mold. Cover with aluminum foil and place in a baking pan. Carefully add warm water to the pan until it comes 1 inch up the sides of the pudding mold.

5 CUPS FRESH SOUR CHERRIES, PITTED

¾ CUP SUGAR

1 CUP CHIANTI

3 Place the pan in the preheated oven and bake for 40 minutes. Remove the foil and cook for 20 more minutes, until the pudding is firm.

4 Meanwhile, make the cherry sauce: place the cherries in a sauté pan over medium heat. Add the sugar and bring to a boil. Cook for 2 to 3 minutes, then add the wine. Raise the heat to high and let the alcohol evaporate, about 2 minutes, then remove the cherries with a slotted spoon and reduce the sauce for 5 more minutes. Add the sauce to the cherries.

5 Unmold the pudding onto a plate and serve with the cherry sauce poured over the top.

FARRO PUDDING

SERVES 6 TO 8

IL CLASSICO

Rice pudding is a familiar dessert but unfortunately one that's often soggy and bland.

LA MIA VERSIONE

Making rice pudding with farro gives it a firm, earthy base that's a solid foundation for other big flavors like maple syrup, raisins soaked in Vin Santo, and brown sugar. Unlike the other farro dishes in the book, this one should only be made with firm, nutty, authentic Italian farro.

1½ CUPS FARRO, SOAKED IN COLD WATER OVERNIGHT AND DRAINED

3 CUPS WHOLE MILK

1 CUP HEAVY CREAM

2 TABLESPOONS UNSALTED BUTTER, MELTED

⅓ CUP MAPLE SYRUP

3 LARGE EGGS

¼ CUP PACKED LIGHT BROWN SUGAR PLUS 1 TABLESPOON FOR DUSTING THE SURFACE OF THE PUDDING

¼ CUP RAISINS, SOAKED IN VIN SANTO (SEE PAGE 205) AND DRAINED

¼ CUP PINE NUTS

BUTTER FOR GREASING THE MOLD

1 Preheat the oven to 275°F.

2 Place the farro in a large mixing bowl.

3 In another bowl, whisk together the milk, cream, melted butter, syrup, eggs, and ¼ cup brown sugar and pour this mixture over the farro. Stir well, then stir in the raisins and pine nuts.

4 Transfer this mixture to a heavy ovenproof mold greased with butter. Bake for 30 minutes. Sprinkle the top with 1 tablespoon brown sugar, the raise the heat to 300°F and bake until set, 30 to 40 minutes.

5 Remove from the oven and let cool before serving.

CITRUS ZEST AND ALMOND BISCOTTI

___

MAKES ABOUT 4 DOZEN COOKIES

IL CLASSICO

Biscotti, the Italian cookies born to be dunked in espresso or cappuccino, are classically made plain or with almonds or other nuts.

LA MIA VERSIONE

This recipe produces a tantalizing new variation of biscotti with the refreshing flavor of orange, lime, and lemon zest.

1¼ CUPS BLANCHED ALMONDS

¾ CUP GRANULATED SUGAR

1 TABLESPOON GRATED ORANGE ZEST

1 TABLESPOON GRATED LIME ZEST

1 TABLESPOON GRATED LEMON ZEST

1 CUP CONFECTIONERS' SUGAR, PLUS MORE FOR DUSTING THE WORK SURFACE AND COOKIES

1 TABLESPOON EGG WHITE

1 Preheat the oven to 325°F.

2 Place the almonds and granulated sugar in the bowl of a food processor fitted with the metal blade and process just until coarse crumbs are formed. Transfer to a bowl and stir in the orange, lime, and lemon zest and the confectioners' sugar, mixing thoroughly. Add the egg white and mix with an electric mixer until well blended and firm but not too dry.

3 Dust a work surface with confectioners' sugar. Roll the dough into small logs, about ¾ inch in diameter, and cut them crosswise into 1-inch pieces. Roll each piece into the shape of a ball, then dust it in confectioners' sugar.

4 Line a cookie sheet with parchment paper and place the cookies, 1½ inches apart, on the sheet. Bake until golden outside and soft inside, about 20 minutes. Remove from the oven and let cool on a rack until hardened.

DRIED FRUIT TART

SERVES 8

IL CLASSICO

Panforte (the name means "strong bread") is a dense cake made with dried fruits that is a specialty of Siena enjoyed mostly at the holidays.

LA MIA VERSIONE

This variation on panforte stays true to the ingredients of a traditional one but is fashioned as a tart rather than a cake. Note that you need to soak the pine nuts overnight before proceeding with the rest of the recipe. The dough can also be prepared the day before you plan to bake the tart.

2¼ CUPS ALL-PURPOSE FLOUR, PLUS MORE FOR DUSTING THE WORK SURFACE

8 TABLESPOONS (1 STICK) UNSALTED BUTTER PLUS 1 TEASPOON FOR GREASING THE TART PAN

PINCH OF FINE SEA SALT

1¼ CUPS PINE NUTS

1½ OUNCES SOCIAL TEA OR MARIE COOKIES

1½ CUPS BLANCHED ALMONDS

6 TABLESPOONS SUGAR

9 MEDIUM DRIED FIGS

3 OUNCES PITTED DATES

½ CUP RAISINS

8 LARGE EGG YOLKS

1 TEASPOON GROUND CINNAMON

2 TABLESPOONS CHOPPED CANDIED ORANGE AND LEMON ZEST

9 TABLESPOONS UNSALTED BUTTER, MELTED

DOUGH

1 Place the flour, 1 stick butter, 2 tablespoons cold water, and the salt in a stand mixer and process until amalgamated.

2 Turn out onto a work surface dusted with flour. Form the dough into a ball, wrap it in plastic wrap, and refrigerate for about an hour or overnight.

FILLING AND ASSEMBLY

1 Soak the pine nuts overnight in cold water, then drain and place in the bowl of a food processor with the cookies, almonds, sugar, figs, dates, and raisins. Process together, then turn out into a bowl and add the egg yolks, cinnamon, chopped candied zest, and melted butter. Mix well.

2 Preheat the oven to 350°F.

3 Roll the dough out to form a sheet about ⅛ inch thick.

4 Grease an 11-inch tart pan with a removable bottom with the 1 teaspoon butter. Place the dough over the pan and press to make it conform to the pan.

5 Turn the filling out into the tart pan, cover with aluminum foil, and bake for 30 minutes. Remove the foil and bake for 15 more minutes. Remove from the oven and let cool before serving.

index